ONCE UPON A TIME

ONCE UPON A TIME

A Guide to Moral Decision Making

Dick Hanson

Cover by Allyssa Bean

Scripture taken from the King James Version of the Bible.

Archway Publishing books may be ordered through booksellers or by contacting:

Archway Publishing
1663 Liberty Drive
Bloomington, IN 47403
www.archwaypublishing.com
1 (888) 242-5904

ISBN: 978-1-4808-3886-4 (sc)
ISBN: 978-1-4808-3887-1 (e)

Library of Congress Control Number: 2016917620

Print information available on the last page.

Archway Publishing rev. date: 11/11/2016

CONTENTS

LIST OF ILLUSTRATIONS

ARTICLES OF FAITH

The Church of Jesus Christ of Latter-Day Saints

We believe in God, the Eternal Father, and in His Son, Jesus Christ, and in the Holy Ghost.

- We believe that men will be punished for their own sins, and not for Adam's transgression.
- We believe that through the Atonement of Christ, all mankind may be saved, by obedience to the laws and ordinances of the Gospel.
- We believe that the first principles and ordinances of the Gospel are: first, Faith in the Lord Jesus Christ; second, Repentance; third, Baptism by immersion for the remission of sins; fourth, Laying on of hands for the gift of the Holy Ghost.
- We believe that a man must be called of God, by prophecy, and by the laying on of hands by those who are in authority, to preach the Gospel and administer in the ordinances thereof.
- We believe in the same organization that existed in the Primitive Church, namely, apostles, prophets, pastors, teachers, evangelists, and so forth.
- We believe in the gift of tongues, prophecy, revelation, visions, healing, interpretation of tongues, and so forth.
- We believe the Bible to be the word of God as far as it is translated correctly; we also believe the Book of Mormon to be the word of God.
- We believe all that God has revealed, all that He does now reveal, and we believe that He will yet reveal many great and important things pertaining to the Kingdom of God.
- We believe in the literal gathering of Israel and in the restoration of the Ten Tribes; that Zion (the New Jerusalem) will be built upon the American continent; that Christ will reign personally upon the earth; and, that the earth will be renewed and receive its paradisiacal glory.

- We claim the privilege of worshiping Almighty God according to the dictates of our own conscience, and allow all men the same privilege, let them worship how, where, or what they may.
- We believe in being subject to kings, presidents, rulers, and magistrates, in obeying, honoring, and sustaining the law.
- We believe in being honest, true, chaste, benevolent, virtuous, and in doing good to all men; indeed, we may say that we follow the admonition of Paul-We believe all things, we hope all things, we have endured many things, and hope to be able to endure all things. If there is anything virtuous, lovely, or of good report or praiseworthy, we seek after these things.

FOREWORD

Moral Decision Making

"Statesmen, my dear Sir, may plan and speculate for Liberty, but it is Religion and Morality alone, which can establish the Principles upon which Freedom can securely stand." John Adams in letter to Zabdiel Adams 1776

Morality is a system of rules and behaviors associated with a religious code of conduct. For the purpose of my book I will be using the Judeo-Christian values that the founding fathers based the establishment of the United States government on. The values associated with the Scriptures would be something that all Christian groups could share as they interact with one another. Though there may be some disagreements upon particular verses in the Bible, the overall meaning of moral behavior is generally considered to be agreed-upon. By relying upon the text of the Scriptures we can avoid the temptation to listen to moral philosophers or other human interpretations. As we attempt to define moral standards it is helpful to have the facts as the Scriptures defined them in as was evident in the teachings and life of Jesus Christ.

This system which we are using is different from the idea of situational ethics, which tends to allow decision-making to be based upon the situation that one finds himself in and not in any fixed law. If each of us were to decide which of God's law we wanted to break or disobey it would allow any excuse to be valid. There would be no reason for repentance or following any of the Commandments.

We are confronted every day with moral decisions. In this topsy-turvey world we live in we are bombarded every day in the media, both oral and written, about decisions that affect our nation, our personal lives, and our freedoms. Without some standards or guidelines we can see how some decisions could have an adverse effect upon us, especially since the government has repeatedly interfered in our lives affecting our liberties and rights.

When the founding fathers wrote that the freedom of life liberty and the pursuit of happiness come from God they understood that these sacred truths be honored by the government that was established. Sometimes the common good for all people is discarded and we see gross injustices applied to certain groups. Under attack in today's world is religious freedom, family unity, and the definition of marriage. So we must ask ourselves if we are willing to turn over these sacred rights to those who would subjugate us to a standard of behavior that is not consistent with the moral principles taught by the Savior.

I leave you then with this quote by Gouverneur Morris, he said," religion is the only solid base of morals and morals are the only possible support of free governments." Letter to George Gordon 1792

Acknowledgements

First, I would like to thank my wife Nancy for her continued support in this endeavor to write my second book. Next, my children, who are the love of my life, and have been an inspiration to me, have always encouraged my projects.

To my daughter Heather, who did the editing and review of the manuscript which is critical to success.

To Molly, Jason, Pete, and Erik (deceased) , my great children.

To Alyssa Bean, an art teacher, who provided the excellent drawings to go with each chapter, I give my heartfelt thanks, and my granddaughter Gemma who also added some drawings.

Finally, I acknowledge the Spirit which provides the insight and inspiration needed to produce a work on this important topic.

INTRODUCTION

Never before in the history of America has there been a more critical time to revisit the idea of making moral decisions. It seems that whatever venue one observes, there is a blatant attack on moral values. This is true in athletics, from youth up to the professional arena; in politics at virtually every level; in Hollywood and other areas of entertainment; in business; and right down to the personal level of everyday behavior.

The United States of America is a country that was established with a firm position on religion and morality. The declaration of independence provided the foundation for a belief in God and the rights of man. There was the principle that God's laws are supreme to the laws of man. These fundamental beliefs provided the framework for the development of the Constitution and were woven through the tapestry of America's history. In our day, it seems the tapestry has been tattered and torn by the introduction of principles that were not consistent to the beliefs of the founding fathers.

I will endeavor to explain, through a series of short essays, why I believe that moral decision-making is a critical need in our day. I have used stories, fables, poetry, and events to make the point that there is a set of moral rules and a code of conduct that God has introduced to all mankind that, if followed, will bring us back to a high standard of moral behavior.

"Once upon a time" was a phrase that was used at the beginning of fables, fairy tales, some poetry, and other literary sources that had a moral concept at the end of each work. There was always a lesson learned that introduced the act of choosing right or wrong

Chapter 1

THE ALBATROSS

At length did cross an albatross, Thorough the fog it came;
As if it had been a Christian soul, we hailed it in God's name.

—Samuel Taylor Coleridge
From "The Rime of the Ancient Mariner"

In the epic poem "The Rime of the Ancient Mariner," by Samuel Taylor Coleridge, a seabird called an albatross was a good omen for all men at sea. In the story, the ancient mariner decides to shoot down the albatross. He says, "Why look'st thou so? With my crossbow I shot the albatross." His shipmates are concerned that they will have bad luck for the rest of their journey because of this unfortunate act. So they take matters into their own hands. The mariner says, "Instead of a cross, the albatross about my neck was hung."

From that time forward, to have an albatross around the neck has meant to have a burden placed upon us. Sometimes this burden is brought about by the decisions we make. It may be that others cause us to have undue hardships, or we may face problems just in the everyday living of life.

Whatever the reason we find ourselves with undue hardship, there is always hope that we can alleviate the problem by using good moral decision-making. It requires of us to have hope and a firm resolve to remedy the situation.

Some of the problems we face because of poor decision-making may include addiction to drugs, alcohol, tobacco, sexual misconduct, or pornography. As serious as these may seem, there is a way out, through moral decision-making. This may require us to go through some form of rehabilitation, counseling, or other forms of help via friends, ecclesiastical leaders, medical professionals, or other trained personnel. It will not be easy, nor will it be a matter of short-term fixes. If we understand the principles that we are children of God, that we have a purpose here in life, that we are loved, and that we have the opportunity to become better people, then the journey we must make will give us a sense of meaning and accomplishment and will enrich our lives. We can change by using the God-given gift of agency. It will not be easy, but it will be rewarding. Once we understand the power of agency, we will be able to use it to enhance our decision-making and see the results of our moral choices.

If our afflictions are caused by what others do to us, it will be our obligation to learn how to forgive. This is not an easy task because of our determination to judge others harshly. Therefore, we must learn what the Savior taught throughout his life here on earth. If we believe that there is no trial without a way to be able to get through it, then we start on the road to understanding the Savior's teaching on true forgiveness. The Savior's code of conduct, taught throughout the Scriptures, give us a framework for behavior, enables us to develop trust in him, and allows us to show mutual respect for all people. He will be the provider of justice and mercy to those who learn how to forgive.

Throughout our lives we may be faced with trials and tribulations. These may include illness, the death of a friend or family member, a debilitating accident, or the loss of possessions. We may suffer from a bitter divorce, or a wayward child, or the loss of a job. In order to not only survive but to come out ahead, we will need the ability to make good moral and ethical decisions. This requires a deep and abiding faith in Jesus Christ and the application of atonement in our lives.

All of these situations and circumstances which may befall us require us to have a solid framework in making moral and ethical decisions. We may need to avoid places that offer temptations, stop associating with people who would want to bring us down, or fill our minds with good thoughts by watching/listening to wholesome movies and music. Throughout this book I will give examples to show you how and why these decisions are so important to understand and to apply in our lives. At the end of each chapter, I will give examples of people who have applied these types of decisions in their lives as they have gone through their own trials and tribulations. I have also provided helpful scriptures that will answer some important questions and provide insight into our quest to make good choices.

As a personal example, I want to share with you an experience I had when I returned home from Vietnam after the loss of my right arm. I was stationed at Valley Forge Army Hospital in Pennsylvania. The soldiers there were going through rehabilitation while we were still in the service, waiting to be either discharged or reassigned. Those of us who were ambulatory had to get up each morning, make our beds, shave, have breakfast, and report to our assigned jobs. I was given a job in the library, where I worked each day. Of course we were able to go to therapy and other medical treatment as needed. Once a week each hospital ward, including all soldiers., was brought to a large room with a circle of chairs, where we sat and waited to be called to a chair in the middle of the circle. Once there, the doctor would come up and explain the injuries of each soldier and what they had done to help deal with the particular wound. The important lesson I learned from this experience was being made to feel less self-conscious about my injury, but more importantly, it gave me the opportunity to see others who were worse off than I was. I was reluctant to complain about my situation, because I knew I could live a relatively normal life.

After being discharged from Valley Forge, I was assigned to a VA hospital for inpatient care and then eventually as an outpatient. At home, I had the love and support of my family, friends, and ecclesiastical leaders. The adjustment took time, but eventually I returned to college, where I got my degree. Along the way, the moral decisions that I made gave me a deeper insight into life's challenges and how to overcome them.

Example 1: The first example I want to use is that of former first lady Betty Ford. She was an alcoholic and hooked on prescription drugs. She was in denial for a while, until her family intervened. After coming to the realization that she was an addict, she became a great spokesman for others with similar problems. She opened the Betty Ford Center, based on the twelve steps of Alcoholics Anonymous, where others could come for help. In 2003 she also published a book that dealt with her story.

Example 2: The second example I want to use is that of Helen Keller. She was born with both deafness and blindness. Under the tutelage of a great teacher, Anne Sullivan, Helen was able to overcome her disabilities and go on to help improve the way society treated deaf people. She learned to read Braille and eventually went on to get a college degree.

Scripture References

Genesis: 1:26–28; Matthew 26:39; 2 Corinthians 7:10; Acts 17:29; Proverbs 3:5–6; Doctrine and Covenants 136:21

Chapter 2

THE BEATITUDES

And he opened His mouth and taught them, saying,

—Matthew 5:2

In the fifth chapter of Matthew, the Savior went up on a mountain and taught his disciples what are known today as the Beatitudes. These give us some insight into how we are to conduct our lives and be able to make the moral decisions that the Savior taught.

The first teaching He gave was this: "Blessed are the poor in spirit: for theirs is the kingdom of heaven." What does it mean to be poor in spirit? The Savior suggests that we come unto him with a broken heart and a contrite spirit. This means a sense of humility and a willingness to repent of our wrongdoings and come unto the Savior, willing to obey his commandments and to lean on him for our refuge. We understand that he has a place reserved for those who are truly trying to become his disciples. What greater reward to those who are faithful than to have a place in the kingdom of heaven?

The second teaching he gave was "Blessed are they that mourn: for they shall be comforted." How many of us have gone through a time of grief, sorrow, or mourning over the death of a friend or relative? This is a natural part of our mortal existence. But the Savior—who won the victory over death and experienced in the garden of Gethsemane all of our pain, suffering, and agony and bore our sins upon him—is the one who can understand completely our suffering. Again, the moral decision to put our faith and trust in the Lord can help us through these troubling times. Several years ago, my family and I lost a son and brother to the addictive power of drugs and alcohol. He became so distraught that he took his own life. Our understanding of, and faith in, the gospel of Jesus Christ taught us that he can still be a part of our eternal family. We do not always understand the meaning of a tragedy that happens, but we can have confidence that the Savior does. Our son is in the spirit world, where he will be taught the gospel free from his mortal body, which had become addicted to his unwise choices.

There is always hope and a sure knowledge that the Savior can and will provide that true balm in Gilead.

The Savior then taught, "Blessed are the meek: for they shall inherit the earth." Meekness and humility go hand in hand; they require us to be submissive to the will of the Savior and to be teachable. He is willing to bring us to a point in our lives where we can learn of his doctrine and know for a surety that he loves us and wants us to be successful. How many of us over the years of going through the formal education process have come in contact with a great teacher—a teacher who understood us, knew of our potential, and had the ability to bring it out? This teacher also taught us by example and at times was hard on us in order to make us stretch and grow. How much more do you think the Savior could teach us if we were willing to submit to the laws and ordinances of the gospel? He was the greatest motivator and teacher of all time. The moral decision to be teachable is within our grasp.

Next the Savior taught, "Blessed are they which do hunger and thirst after righteousness: for they shall be filled." We have all had times, I'm sure, when we were hungry and thirsty in the physical sense of the terms. There are many people throughout the world who live every day facing hunger and thirst, and in some cases even starvation. There is much we can do to alleviate these physical problems, and we do this through the generous donations of food, shelter, water, medical supplies, and other types of aid. But the Savior was talking about us becoming hungry and thirsty after the word of God. We do that by reading and studying the Scriptures. Our goal should be to immerse ourselves in the word of God, in which we can find answers to all of our problems. We learn that it is our duty, responsibility, and privilege to help others receive the physical needs they are seeking. The other responsibility we have, which the Savior taught, is to go throughout the world teaching repentance and baptism in bringing people into the gospel. It takes moral courage to be a disciple of the Savior as we hunger and thirst after righteousness, knowing that we are not perfect; yet studying, praying, and pondering the Scriptures will bring us closer to him.

Next the Savior taught, "Blessed are the merciful: for they shall obtain mercy." Who can deny that in our day and time there is much need for the idea of mercy? We hear a cacophony of voices shouting, yelling, noisemaking, accusing, ridiculing, and offering a host of other insults. In an article he wrote called "New Crisis is Coming," Thomas Sowell, a conservative professor, mentioned that an old-time trial lawyer once said to him, "When your case is weak, shout louder!" We see and hear so much of that today, throughout all segments of society. It seems that mercy and forgiveness are lost in the loud rhetoric of vitriolic speech.

Do mercy and forgiveness have a place in our lives? If we look at the Savior and see how many times he extended mercy and forgiveness to those who were sinners, we see the only one who can truly forgive; this is an example to use in our own lives. After his experience in the garden of Gethsemane, you will remember, one of his disciples cut off an ear from one of the soldiers. The Savior immediately healed this man, even after the agony he had just gone through. A woman caught in adultery was extended forgiveness, a lesson we should all learn about casting the first stone. On the cross he hung, suffering physical pain, and yet he counseled his brother to look after his mother. Before his final breath he pleaded with God, saying, "Forgive them, for they know not what they do."

In our system of laws and legality, sometimes the innocent are convicted, and sometimes the guilty go free; nonetheless, the system does a fairly good job. How much more will the Savior's law, which is perfect, provide? Justice and mercy will be served. He will be the final judge of all of our lives, and though it seems as if people get away with these doings, in the end, no one will be exempt from his judgment.

Next, the Savior said, "Blessed are the pure in heart: for they shall see God." To be pure in heart means to acknowledge that there is a God in the universe and that he has an eternal plan for each of us, his sons and daughters. By following his plan, we are able to develop an inner peace, knowing for a surety that the good we do in this life will be what our heavenly father wants us to do. What a great blessing it is to have what the Bible calls "the peace that passes understanding." Obtaining peace for ourselves enables us to pass it on to others. Again it requires us to make a moral decision to follow God, obey his commandments, and eventually to try to become more like he is.

His next teaching was stated as "Blessed are the peacemakers: for they shall be called the children of God." Is anything more vital to the people of this earth than to have peace? The world is in commotion and has been since the beginning of time. Anger, argument, greed, and lust for power and control are Satan's tools to keep constant uproar and contention among men. We know that in the last days there will be wars and rumors of wars. Having been involved in the Vietnam War, I know firsthand how destructive conflicts can be. War is devastating in the amount of life, property, and resources that are destroyed. But it is no different than arguing and bickering among ourselves, for it leads to the same result. The Savior taught that we are to love everyone, including our enemies. He was the great peacemaker, and he gave us guidelines to follow to bring about peace. The moral decision to turn the other cheek and try to understand the power we have to face any opposition and still be Christlike in our actions and in our words will enable us to truly be called peacemakers.

Then the Savior taught, "Blessed are they which are persecuted for righteousness sake: for theirs is the kingdom of heaven. Blessed are ye when men shall revile you, and persecute you, and shall say all manner of evil against you falsely, for my sake. Rejoice, and be exceedingly glad: for great is your reward in heaven." These are powerful words that may seem impossible to live by. How can we be glad of persecution? How can we rejoice if we are falsely accused or if someone says or does something to hurt or humiliate us? The ultimate moral decision here is to come unto Christ, to accept his gospel, to obey the commandments to the best of our ability, to pray fervently, and to know that we can experience the miracle in the change in our lives. I emphasize this: to be able to accomplish these goals, we need to teach the power of moral decision-making. Our decisions will be based on a code of conduct, a set of rules, an eternal plan, and Christian standards that can be found in the Holy Scriptures.

Example 1: William Wilberforce was an antislavery politician who lived in England during the mid-1700's and early 1800'. His fierce desire to end slavery became his lifelong goal. A Christian man, he abstained from alcohol and wasted little time in socializing with the other politicians. He also was a force for high moral standings and conduct. He was a great philanthropist and helped form many groups that aided the poor. He would not surrender his ideas, though he came under much opposition and fierce criticism.

Example 2: Joan of Arc was the daughter of an English farmer; she was not taught to read or write. She did have instilled in her a deep love for the church and its teachings. At the age of thirteen, she felt she had been given a mission to help save France. Her story is remarkable in the fact that this young woman was able to lead the army and win many important battles. Her story reflects once again the moral decision-making and Christian virtues that formed an integral part of her life.

Scriptures: Matthew 5: 1–12, 2 Corinthians 7:10; Proverbs 16:32; Proverbs 23:7

Chapter 3

CHIVALRY/CIVILITY

Some say the age of chivalry is past, that the spirit of romance is dead. The age of chivalry is never past, so long as there is a wrong left unredressed on earth.

—Charles Kingsley

During the Middle Ages, there was a system of virtues and qualities represented in our literature that was instituted by the knights. Certain orders of chivalry appeared to produce sanctification of its members and to protect religious peoples from their enemies. Its members took vows and made commitments. This included, but was not limited to, men who acted nobly and honorably and who showed great respect to the ladies of that day.

As these knights perfected their skills of strength in combat, they were also expected to act under a code, which they agreed to honor. Under the code they had to fear God, to serve with valor, to take care of widows, to obey authority, to keep the faith, to speak the truth at all times, and to respect and honor women. Other qualities included temperance, diligence, prudence, and resoluteness.

Most of the qualities mentioned above required years of training and service as a squire, practicing not only the art of war but of developing the moral judgment needed to become a true knight.

Can you imagine if our elected officials today had the same duty of developing these qualities and attributes? They would not focus their service on power, prestige, or the honor men but rather on the people they are indebted to. Of course, the desirability of these characteristics is not limited to those in government service but is equally important to men and women in all vocations of life. This again requires the moral decision-making skill that is so lacking in our society. This way of life need not confine itself to the age of knights in shining armor riding gallantly on horseback and wielding the sword of justice and the lance of honor. In our intemperate society, each of us needs to develop this lifestyle of honor and integrity. It would be tremendously beneficial if we were all courteous, kind, understanding, and honorable in all of our dealings. Likewise, we need a sense of civility in our daily words, deeds, actions, and interactions with others. How much violence could we avoid if we toned down our rhetoric and accusatory manner of language? Speech can be a powerful soother, or it can be a divisive tool. Remember the verse in Proverbs that says, "A soft answer turns away wrath."

"There can be no high civility without a deep morality," said Ralph Waldo Emerson.

We are living at a time when rudeness seems to prevail. The use of profanity, character assassination, unprecedented negative political campaigns, and uncontrolled mass demonstrations seem to be the norm. The responsibility of undoing this negativity begins with the individual. Then it extends to the family unit, into our neighborhoods, our towns and cities, and finally to our states and country. As individuals, we need to start making the moral decisions to be courteous and kind in our relationships with family and friends.

As a former educator, I can attest to the fact that students, for the most part, learn to be disrespectful to teachers and administrators because of what they have learned in their homes. Instruction in the art of etiquette and manners should be reintroduced as an integral part of early childhood education. There needs to be a moral and religious revival that permeates all of society. There are many religious groups that do much good in the area of teaching standards of behavior and conduct. However, as noted previously, the attack on the family, church, and marriage has had a negative impact on life in America. The elimination of prayer in schools, the suggestion we stop reading the Pledge of Allegiance and displaying any Christian symbolism on public property have taken the meaning of "separation of church and state" out of context.

The whole basis for civility can be found within a biblical framework. Christ's injunctions to love our neighbor as ourselves and to love our enemies and do good to those that harm us are not just idle words but rather a way of life that each of us can attain by our efforts to make moral decisions. Our speech, our demeanor, our actions, our deeds, and our interactions with others will tell a lot about our characters as disciples of Christ.

Alexis de Tocqueville, a French political scientist and historian, who lived in the 1800's once said, "The health of the democratic society may be measured by the quality of functions performed by private citizens." The famed historian and political scientist also said, "The Americans combine the notions of religion and liberty so intimately in their minds that it is impossible to make them conceive of one without the other." In his book *Democracy in America* he expounded these thoughts and many others about how great the American system of democracy was, as it adhered to the religious principles authored by the founding fathers.

The Dalai Lama once said, "Our prime purpose in this life is to help others. If you can't help them, at least don't hurt them."

Mahatma Gandhi once said, "My life is my message." If we can take the words of these great men and incorporate them into our lives, then we can truly say that the age of chivalry and civility is not over but will live on because of the way we conduct our lives.

Example 1: Mahatma Gandhi led the nonviolent movement for independence in India even though he was jailed several times for his protests.

Example 2: Dalai Lama was a great spiritual and political leader of the Tibetan people who led the nonviolent resistance to the Chinese who were trying to rule Tibet.

Scriptures: Matthew 7:12, 5:46; John 15:13; James 1:26; Ecclesiasts 10:12; 3 Nephi 27:27

Chapter 4

FIDDLER ON THE ROOF

Tradition, tradition. Without our traditions, our lives would be as shaky as a fiddler on the roof!

—Tevye

Joseph Stein's book *Fiddler on the Roof*, which became a big-hit musical on Broadway, depicts the story of a Jewish family living in a *shtetl* that was subject to the Russian bureaucracy. The main character, Tevye, a philosophical village milkman, explains throughout the story how Jewish traditions have shaped and molded the lives of the people in the small village of Anatevka.

My purpose in using this story is to illustrate how people can still use moral decision-making even while living under the rule of an oppressive government. I also want to examine the idea of traditions that are an integral part of religious life for both Christians and Jews.

A lot of the Jews in Eastern Europe at that time lived in small towns called shtetls. Most of these were market towns where residents traded goods or services. These communities were governed by a Jewish council called *kahal*. The major values of these communities were, of course, the Jewish religion and the people's humanness. Living the life of a good Jew was important; it was reflected in the way they worshiped in the synagogue and the way they treated each other with respect and justice and admired scholarly learning. The synagogue to the Jew was a house of worship and study as well as an assembly hall. The Jewish rabbi, as well as the *yidn*, a group of men of learning and substance, occupied the most important places in the synagogue.

To the Jews living in the small hamlets, the home was the basic unit, where Jewish culture and traditions were taught. The family was patriarchal in order, and on the Sabbath day the father led the family in their worship service. There the ritual of the Passover meal, or seder, was observed and oft-times it was shared with either strangers or the poor of the community. When the Jews observed bar mitzvahs and weddings, births or deaths, or illness and recovery, it extended out to the community. This is not to say that life in the shtetl was naïvely idyllic, for each place was different from the other. Nevertheless, the sense of cooperation and consideration for every member of the community led them to be quite successful, and they were able to maintain law and order without a police force. Owing to the fact that they were under an oppressive communist government, they still succeeded in keeping their religious faith and their traditions intact. This required a continual attempt to make moral decisions based upon their beliefs. Under such circumstances, Jewish life survived for the most part due to the people's unwavering religious convictions.

As many of the Jews who lived in the small towns were merchants, farmers, peddlers, and artisans, the marketplace was an important part of community life. Here goods and services were exchanged, and it became a meeting place for both the Jews and the non-Jews. Often goods and services were brought in from the larger cities. Financial transactions were not huge, because most of the Jews lived in poverty, and many barely made enough to provide food and clothing for their family members. To buy a chicken or fish for the Sabbath meal was a big accomplishment. Hence, many tried their hands at various trades and occupations.

The existence of these small communities ended in the nineteenth and twentieth centuries as Jews began to migrate out of Eastern Europe. Others were caught in the Holocaust, in which millions were killed. The lessons learned from these groups was that even under extreme circumstances a people could still choose to live according to the values and beliefs and traditions that they so nobly cherished.

> A fiddler on the roof—sounds crazy, no? But here, in our little village of Anatevka, you might say every one of us is a fiddler on the roof trying to scratch out a pleasant, simple life without breaking his neck. It isn't easy. You may ask, "Why do we stay here if it's so dangerous?" Well, we stay because Anatevka is our home. And how do we keep our balance? That I can tell you in one word: tradition!

> —Tevye
> From *Fiddler on the Roof*

I would like to share some thoughts now on the idea of traditions of both a religious and a family nature. By observing Christian practices and traditions of religious observance, we are able to make wise decisions when it comes to the moral implications of our actions. In the story we just observed above, the lead character, Tevye, was extremely proud of his traditions but was also able to adapt when a particular one was not suited for consideration. We must be careful to choose wisely between those traditions that are valuable and those that are vain observances.

For our discussion, Christian practices may vary by denomination, but there are some elements that are common to each group. As we observe a Sunday worship service, engage ourselves in private and family prayer, read and study the Scriptures, and participate in rites such as baptism and receiving the gift of the Holy Ghost, we can become more Christlike in our thoughts and interactions.

As a nation, we celebrate specific holidays throughout the year. These include New Year's, Presidents' Day, Martin Luther King Day, Columbus Day, Easter, Memorial Day, Veterans' Day, Thanksgiving, Flag Day, Christmas, Lent, Passover, and others, and we develop a sense of deep admiration and patriotism for this great nation in which we live. The founding fathers developed for us the foundation for a government that was truly for the people and by the people.

In America, traditions and customs come about through areas such as religion, food, clothing, language, behavior, morals, and a host of others. The immigrants who came to this country brought with them some of their own customs and traditions, which many still adhere to today.

For the sake of this book, I am considering the religious views of the Judeo-Christian belief system. In a recent survey, 83 percent of Americans identified themselves as Christians. Therefore, in the area of moral decision-making, I will make the argument using the Scriptures as a guide.

Many families create their own traditions and customs whereby they can teach their children the importance of the American way of life and what it means to worship God. When our children were younger, my wife and I had them participate in a tradition at Christmas time whereby we made various kinds of cookies and loaves of bread shaped like teddy bears. We would allow them to pick a family to deliver these loaves and cookies to. We would also go to the woods and pick out a Christmas tree to take home to decorate. We took our children to church and had them participate in a youth activities associated with it.

Each person then, has to decide which customs and traditions to follow and teach to his or her family. It takes moral courage to follow the dictates of your conscience when it comes to adhering to and practicing religious convictions.

"Within the covers of the Bible are the answers for all the problems men face," said Ronald Reagan

Example 1: William Tyndale was one of the first persons to translate the Bible into English for use by ordinary people. He was executed for blasphemy but never forsook his beliefs.

Example 2: Mother Teresa devoted her life to serving the poor while overcoming poverty, disease, and criticism. Starting in India, she reached out to those in need around the world.

Scriptures: Proverbs 3:3; John 8:32, 14:6; 2 Timothy 3:1–7; 2 Thessalonians 2:15–17; 2 Nephi 2:11; Acts 14:22

Chapter 5

GRIMM'S FAIRY TALES

Once upon a time there was a hermit who lived in the forest at the foot of a mountain, and he passed the time by praying and doing good deeds. To honor God, he would carry several pails of water up the mountainside each evening. Since there was always a hard wind that dried out the air and soil at the mountain peak, many an animal was able to quench its thirst because of the water he carried, and many a plant was refreshed (*The Three Green Twigs*).

What child hasn't been thrilled by the stories of Snow White, Cinderella, Little Red Riding Hood, Hansel and Gretel, and many other fairy tales created by the Grimm brothers? Over the years, some of these have been made into animated movies as well as films using live actors and actresses.

Born and raised in Germany, Jacob and Wilhelm Grimm would listen intently to the storytellers who would go from town the town and tell their tales with such vividness and accuracy. These stories, retold from generation to generation, were filled by the likes of heroes and heroines, witches, giants, dwarfs, and enchanters. The Grimm brothers grabbed hold of these experiences and produced their own version, making it into what is today known as *Grimm's Fairy Tales*. These tales, many of which have a moral ending, have captivated people through the centuries. Let us examine some of these tales and take advantage of the moral truths that are contained within.

Morals and values have always had an impact on people's lives, even in our modern society. Through the use of morals, people tend to justify their action (or their inaction), what they say, and what they do. They also influence the way others perceive them and react to them. Teaching children about morals and values gives them the opportunity to evaluate and recognize those that they regularly come in contact with. Though this teaching is not intended to be about a specific religion, for our purposes, we would try to define those values that are consistent with most Christian denominations. We would hope that after this process we and our children would be able to incorporate these moral values into our lives as circumstances dictate.

Our purpose is to help not only children but adults also to develop higher-order thinking skills as they apply to the concepts of self-awareness, honesty, cooperation, respect, trustworthiness, and fairness. Let us begin by examining some of the phrases that are found in these fairy tales:

Actions speak louder than words. I remember once hearing an anonymous quote that went like this: "One is not what one says he is but what one demonstrates himself to be." It is easy to *say* things, but sometimes it's a little bit harder to actually *do* them. With the political situation the way it is in America today, we hear so much rhetoric and promises but not enough actual results that would benefit the people. It is so easy for politicians to say the right things to the crowds, but it is much harder to actually demonstrate the ideas and policies when a person is more concerned with personal power and authority.

Don't judge a book by its cover. Glamour and beauty and clothing styles permeate the media so completely that it has become obsessive, especially in the Hollywood crowd. Outward appearance seems to be the most important thing to certain groups of people and their followers. As children of God, we are each unique and acceptable in his eyes. He is more concerned with the inner qualities that really determine who we are. Self-awareness is something we develop by understanding our true inner natures and not by any outward appearance. Remember, each of us has talents and abilities, strengths and weaknesses, but our characters are developed by our inner commitment to make good judgments.

Every cloud has a silver lining. Sleeping Beauty eventually found her Prince Charming after suffering some setbacks in her life. Once we understand who we are and what we have the potential to become, and we realize that we have the power to overcome any difficulty, we can look forward to our rewards in heaven. Trials and tribulations can have a positive or negative effect upon us. We can use them to develop a stronger desire to overcome bitterness and forlornness. Remember that the Savior of the world overcame all trials, pain, and suffering such as we cannot fathom. He is willing, then, to succor us and help strengthen our resolve to come to him.

In our age of technological advances, it is refreshing to know that we can still benefit from the age-old ideas of fairy tales, stories, and other literary mediums that teach great moral principles. If there is a greater need in our society than to have people making moral and ethical decisions, then I don't know what it would be. The ability to make analogies between good and evil, to find discrepancies between what is right and wrong, to discourage bad habits, and to develop the attributes we discussed above will help us along our journeys to discover the importance of moral decision-making within the parameters of good Christian living.

Example 1: Jacob and Wilhelm Grimm developed and published their great volume of fairy tales.

Example 2: Aesop was a slave and storyteller who lived in ancient Greece and produced what we know today as Aesop's fables, another selection of stories with moral endings.

Scriptures: The parables of Jesus in the New Testament; 1 Nephi 1:6–35

HANSON HOMESTEAD   1940-1954
82 RINGWOOD AVE. POMPTON LAKES, N.J.

Chapter 6

HOUSE TO HOME

It takes a heap o' livin' in a house t' make it home.

—Edgar Guest

This line from Edgar Guest's immortal poem entitled "Home" sets the theme for this chapter. In twenty-first-century America, the family and the concept of home has come under relentless attack. Marriage is no longer defined as a union between one man and one woman. Why is this such an important idea to examine and determine the real meaning of?

People live in all kinds of houses. Some are fine and elegant, some are shabby and poor, and some are in between these two extremes. But the families that reside within them are the focus of our discussion. Stephen Covey once said, "When it comes to developing character strength, inner security, and unique personal and interpersonal talents and skills in a child, no institution can, or ever will, compare with, or effectively substitute for, the homes' potential for positive influence." Too many of today's children do not have the experience of the traditional home wherein resides a mother, a father, and children. This is not to say that children outside of these conditions cannot grow up to be fine, upstanding citizens—but the chances are substantially reduced.

There have been numerous studies which show a direct correlation between a child's success at school and the family environment from which the child comes. There is a famous quote from Strickland Gillilan that says, "You may have tangible wealth untold, caskets of jewels and coffers of gold. Richer than I you can never be—I had a mother who read to me." There's a lot to be said about this quote. Since two-parent families have been on the decline in recent years, we can see the effect it has on our children. Coupled with that decline is the fact that unwed childbirths are on the rise. We can find through empirical studies the effect this has on the children. What is the positive effect for children who come from two-parent families? We know that their readiness for school improves greatly, especially children whose parents read to them when they were very young. These children show less aggression and anxiety and tend to have higher reading-achievement scores. They tend to be more engaged in the school experience and exhibit higher academic success. I could go on, with a list many studies that have been done on the effects on children of coming from other-than-traditional families. You and I know that so much of this is just common sense. When we make the moral decision to act in accordance with God's plan in relation to family structure, we reap the rewards intended for obeying his laws. A quote from the Church of Jesus Christ of Latter-day Saints' proclamation on the family says, "The family is ordained of God. Marriage between man and woman is essential to his eternal plan. Children are entitled to birth within the bond of matrimony and to be reared by a father and a mother who honor marital vows with complete fidelity." I'm sure you will hear many arguments to dispute the fact that marriage between a man and woman is a part of God's plan. But facts are stubborn things. We can see the results of a divergence from this plan—society becomes disorganized and eventually could fall into complete disarray.

Amelia Earhart once said, "The more one does and sees and feels, the more one is able to do, and the more genuine may be one's appreciation of fundamental things like home, and love, and understanding companionship."

Oliver Wendell Holmes once said, "Where we love is home—home that our feet may leave, but not our hearts."

Finally, Confucius has said, "The strength of a nation derives from the integrity of the home."

In this day of great technological advances and an ever-increasing knowledge of worldly things, we must still be sensitive to the calm reassurance that comes from following God's law. Since the world began, the family has been the institution established as a basis for personal life. Throughout every culture and nation, the family unit is the most revered. It is the foundation upon which nations are built and upon which true happiness is found. In no place is moral decision-making more needed, more important for society, than in the area of marriage and family. We are a Christian nation, and we need to follow the eternal truths on this important subject as founded in the Holy Scriptures.

Example 1: Theodore Roosevelt and Nellie May Hanson, my parents, who gave me my first home. Though they separated, they never divorced, and I eventually did the temple work where vicarious ordinances such as baptism and confirmation are done for deceased family members.

Lester and Dolly Hunt were the uncle and aunt I lived with after my parents separated. They started me going to church in the Presbyterian and Methodist congregations. Their work was also done in the temple.

Example 2: Joseph and Emma Smith, early leaders in the Latter-day Saints movement. They endured many tribulations and trying conditions throught their lives, yet their love remained steadfast and true. Their story is one that should be told over and over again.

Scriptures: 1 Timothy 5:4; Alma 40:11; John 14:1–4

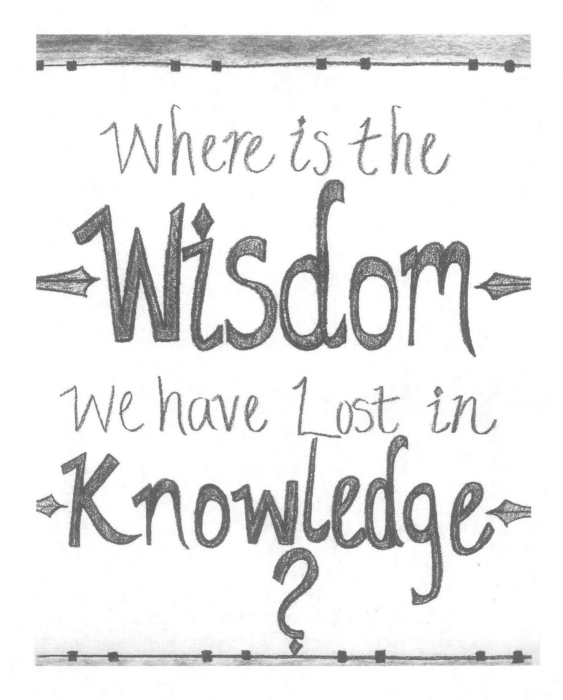

Chapter 7

KNOWLEDGE AND WISDOM

For the Lord giveth wisdom: out of his mouth cometh knowledge and understanding.

—Proverbs 2:6

In this advanced technological age, information comes to us at a remarkable speed. With all this information comes the need to extrapolate truth from fiction. In the political arena, there is much spin, half-truths, lies, and evasion of truth. We have come to understand that for personal gain people will simply ignore facts and say what is expedient for the moment.

Knowledge is a great thing. William Ralph Inge once said, "The aim of education is the knowledge not of facts but of values." That leads us to see how important it is to have values and morals that guide us to knowledge of worth—not only to our minds but to our souls.

T. S. Eliot said, "Where is a life we have lost in living? Where is the wisdom we have lost in knowledge? Where is the knowledge we have lost in the information?"

In 11 Timothy 3:1, 7, it says, "This know also, that in the last days perilous times will come ..." Ever learning, and never able to come to the knowledge of the truth."

These quotes enable us to determine that knowledge is very important, but correct knowledge of who we are and who we are to become is of great worth for us *eternally*. Of course we want people to have knowledge and expertise in their careers. We want doctors who have knowledge of medicine and operational procedures. We want accountants with an understanding of tax laws and proper deductions. We want our auto mechanics to comprehend the workings of an engine. The list could go on and on about how important knowledge is in our everyday lives and for those we associate with. But simply knowing something, without the ability to make moral decisions, is not enough. Our appetites sometimes rule our judgment, in the food we eat or substances we take into our bodies. We know that driving an automobile and trying to text on a cell phone is not the smartest thing to do, but many drivers continue to do it. We also know that disobeying both temporal and spiritual laws can put us in bondage in one form or another. Consider this quote from John Adams: "Let us tenderly and kindly cherish, therefore, the means of knowledge. Let us dare to read, think, speak, and write." We therefore need to get to a higher plane of knowledge. We can do this through the Scriptures, for the Savior taught of the power that comes through knowledge of who he is and what he wants us to become. When he taught in parables, he used everyday examples from the environment in which he lived. These examples taught us the importance of our lives here on earth; they taught about things that have happened in the past and things that will happen in our time. This higher plane of knowledge we will call *wisdom*.

Eleanor Roosevelt once said, "One's philosophy is not best expressed in words; it is expressed in the choices one makes … and the choices we make are ultimately our responsibility." So how does one make this leap from knowledge to wisdom? It may seem impossible at times to be able to differentiate between truth and error. If we believe that God will not give us any challenge that we cannot overcome, this will help us understand that we may make mistakes but we *can* truly and continually become better people.

You may recall a famous quote from Lao Tzu that says, "The journey of a thousand miles begins with one step." It is important to understand that improvement comes line upon line and precept upon precept. Absorbing here a little and there a little, we can learn and can apply this learning to our progress.

John Wooden, the great UCLA basketball coach, taught these truths: "Talent is God-given. Be humble. Fame is man-given. Be grateful. Conceit is self-given. Be careful."

One of the great books of the Bible is the book of Proverbs, and in there we can find a treasure trove of advice that will help us on our journeys to becoming not only knowledgeable but filled with wisdom. For example, Proverbs 3:3 advises, "Let not mercy and truth forsake thee; bind them about thy neck; write them up on the table of thine heart." In ancient times the Jews wore phylacteries around their necks and hands. These were Scriptures written upon parchment and enclosed in small boxes. This enabled people to have these important verses close by and readily available.

If we develop mercy and truth along with the attributes of being kind and generous one to another, it can help us attain the goal of wise judgment. Jim Rohn once said, "Discipline is the bridge between goals and accomplishment."

Proverbs 9:10 tells us, "The fear of the Lord is the beginning of wisdom; and the knowledge of the holy's understanding."

Finally, in Proverbs 4:7, we read, "Wisdom is the principal thing; therefore get wisdom: and with all thy getting get understanding."

Therefore, differentiating between truth and error should be our number-one goal. We know that there are some things that are simply not true and other things that may be partially true. Our adversaries use all sorts of tricks to try to diffuse what are outright lies. In the case of pornography, for example, there are those who say it is normal and doesn't really hurt anybody. However, in sad experience, we have seen people's lives shattered because of this addiction. Because the Church of Jesus Christ of Latter-day Saints teaches against certain lifestyles, it is accused of being intolerant and prejudiced. The Scriptures teach us that in the last days there will be men with evil designs who will try to deceive the people. The Lord has provided several means by which we can overcome deception. Each person is born with the light of Christ, or what we sometimes call conscience. As well, we have the Holy Ghost, which bears record of all truths. We also have at our fingertips the word of God as found in the Scriptures. The Church of Jesus Christ of Latter-day Saints also proclaims to the world that there are modern-day prophets, seers, revelators, and apostles who will help guide us in our day. So, as we seek learning through study and prayer, we can come to an understanding and knowledge of the truth, which in turn can enable us to gain the wisdom needed to make wise moral decisions. Though the journey may be long and arduous, the destination we can achieve is worth the effort to move us along. In closing, I would like to share a poem I wrote years ago. It is called "The Mountaintop."

The Mountaintop
Dick Hanson

I started many years ago to struggle up that hill; a mere lad I was when first I took a spill.

But Mom and Pop would stand stalwart, my help and guide to be; and though I staggered and stumbled, they still encouraged me.

As years passed by, great sweat had poured from my much-weathered brow; and Mom and Pop were also gone, but still I clutched life's plow.

I climbed and crawled, I plodded on to reach my destiny; but a glass behind still found the bottom much too near to me.

Another of life's tragedies had altered my progress; misfortune knocked me o'er the head, my arm was left a mess.

But wait a while, and here he comes; Mr. Opportunity; another chance he grants to me on my life's journey.

An older man now, the way is steep, the path is blocked by rocks; a stick I need, to rest a while; it's hard to bear life shocks.

Oh Mountaintop, you deceiving knave, why should I reach your peak? But Mr. Man, take heed and listen, your mom and pop did speak.

They said it would be easy, life's journey would be gay. They told me, that to reach the top, a man can't use dismay.

So on again to yonder crest, oh just to reach that crest; oh Mountaintop, you fool, you fool, I'll not give up my quest.

But halfway up life's mountain, a graven image stands; I speak now from best chamber, I've exhausted all my plans.

I look down on the pathway now, that twisted not-a-trail. I see I've come the furthest, though certainly not without avail.

To those of you who are climbing up life's long and weary hill; be strong, be wise, be everything, but don't give up your will.

Although we never reach the top, for death's chariot will arrive; not to try, or hope, or dream, is not even to be alive.

Example 1: King Solomon, who wrote the book of Proverbs and gave a blueprint for obtaining knowledge and wisdom.

Example 2: Marie Currie became a leading scientist in the fields of medicine and physics, and she helped discover the x-ray procedure. She used her knowledge and wisdom to help mankind.

Scriptures: Book of Proverbs; Luke 1:77; James 1:5

Chapter 8

Life, Liberty, and the Pursuit of Happiness

We hold these truths to be self-evident: that all men are created equal, that they are endowed by their Creator with certain inalienable rights ...

—The United States Declaration of Independence

There are certain aspects of the Declaration of Independence that make it unique in the annals of established governments. We understand from the opening statement that the founding fathers acknowledged that we are all creatures of God. When we come to this earth, we are all equal in his sight, having been given certain rights as humans that cannot be taken away by any means. Equality, as defined in the document, ensures that all people are entitled to the established rights. "Inalienable rights" cannot be discarded or in any way tampered with. Thus, the reason for the established government is to protect the sacred rights. We also understand that along with rights come responsibilities for ourselves and for others. Let us, then, consider these three cardinal rights of life, liberty and the pursuit of happiness, separately, so we may understand the moral decision needed to protect them.

Alexis de Tocqueville, in his great work *Democracy in America*, said the following: "America is great because she is good. If America ceases to be good, America will cease to be great." As he traveled around America, he stated that America's greatness was found in the various churches and in the pulpits—the fact that the worship of God was an integral part of making America good. With this in mind, it is important for us to remember that life itself comes from God. We are indeed his spirit children, sent to earth to participate in the plan of salvation. Each life is unique and valuable for each person, regardless of how long or short its span of years.

There are times when life has to be taken, such as in protection of one's own life or property. Also, in time of war it may be necessary to take life. Man's inhumanity to man manifests itself in many ways around the world. Nevertheless, we will all be held accountable for our actions. Abortion, for instance has become an important topic in our time because many call it an act of taking life. If we hold to the view that abortion may be considered under the circumstances of rape, incest, or when the life of the mother may be in danger (with the counsel of competent medical and ecclesiastical leadership), the number of abortions would greatly diminish. We hear often of a woman's right to choose what to do with her body. The choice shouldn't come in the act of abortion but should have been made at the time of having sexual relations. There are two people involved in the creation of life, and neither has the sole responsibility of determining whether that life should be terminated, except under the conditions described above.

People have always wondered, what is the purpose of life? The founding fathers understood that this precious gift comes from God and is not to be dealt with lightly. The Dalai Lama claimed, "The purpose of our lives is to be happy." True happiness comes from understanding and following the plan of happiness outlined in the Scriptures, which our heavenly father wants us to know about.

The Chinese philosopher Lao Tzu also said, "Life is a series of natural and spontaneous changes. Don't resist them—that only creates sorrow. Let reality be reality; let things flow naturally forward in whatever way they like." I would add that life has purpose and meaning only in the sense that we understand this purpose and meaning in the context of the Scriptures. Knowing that life comes from God should make us respect and honor it more diligently.

There is a scripture from Leviticus 25:10 inscribed on the Liberty Bell: "Proclaim liberty throughout the land under all the inhabitants thereof."

John Adams once said, "Liberty must at all hazards be supported. We have a right to derive from our maker. But if we had not, our fathers have earned and bought it for us, at the expense of their ease, their estates, their pleasure, and their blood." This concept was so embedded in the thoughts and actions of these great men and women that they were willing to sacrifice all with a proclamation of liberty. It is a concept for every person, regardless of where or how they live. Liberty does not come, however, with unlimited use and power but with a certain restraint. It does not mean that a person can do anything, anytime that he wants. To engage in evil or unlawful endeavors takes away the very liberty that people have. If we are all equal in the eyes of God, and he wants us to be free, we must follow the rules of the godly life. For in keeping the Commandments we can find true happiness, and liberty will abound in our lives. Freedom and liberty come at a price, for much of the world is under the rule of tyrants who disrespect individual rights and especially liberty. Many people do not have a say in how they live, how they move about, or how they can govern their lives. Many are not allowed to pursue their religious convictions, and many are kept in poverty to prevent them from experiencing independence.

Here's something Thomas Jefferson said: "Honor, justice, and humanity forbid us tamely to surrender that freedom which we received from our gallant ancestors, and which our innocent posterity have a right to receive from us."

In our day we are experiencing some loss of liberty. As the government becomes more and more intrusive in our lives—strapping us with undue restraints, enforcing illegal regulations, and keeping millions dependent on it—liberty is not what it once was. Alexis de Tocqueville once said, after visiting America, "Society will develop a new kind of servitude which covers the surface of society with a network of complicated rules, through which the most original minds and the most energetic characters cannot penetrate. It does not tyrannize but it compresses, enervates, extinguishes, and stupefies a people, till each nation is reduced to nothing better than a flock of timid and industrious animals, of which the government is the shepherd." This is a far cry from the Savior's declaration that he is the good Shepherd and we are his sheep. He knows each one of us and has given each of us an opportunity to become like he is and to live once again with him, our heavenly Father. Tyranny, in any government form, robs us of liberty. The gospel sets us free to enjoy true liberty and happiness.

What does it take to make us happy? And how does the pursuit thereof determine the extent of this happiness? Any discussion of true happiness must come from the religious and moral teachings that the founders of our great nation understood and followed. Many people try to find happiness in worldly possessions, or in power, or in position, or even by thinking that somehow, because of their name or rank or social standing, they are better than others. It is amazing to see to what extent people chase the almighty dollar. Even if some succeed in catching it, the chase begins all over, and they find that they can never really obtain what they're looking for, because there is always more to gain.

I have witnessed, and I'm sure you have, peoples around the world who live without the modern conveniences that are afforded to us but who are extremely happy in their conditions. The value of having material possessions is the opportunity it gives us to use philanthropy to help others in need. All that we have is our gifts from God. They are not ours to own; we are mere stewards of these gifts. When we understand that the Savior of the world had really nothing in the way of possessions but had everything in the way of heavenly gifts, then we want to receive heavenly blessings instead of worldly ones. He has given us the opportunity to someday have a mansion in heaven. Meanwhile, here on earth, it is our duty to help ease the burden of those we come in contact with. Albert Einstein once said, "True religion is real living; living with all one's soul, with all one's goodness and righteousness."

Here is what Ronald Reagan had to say: "Within the covers of the Bible are the answers for all the problems men face."

The pursuit of happiness is also included with the right of conscience, meaning that men are able to worship God according to the dictates of this conscience. The right to own property is also intertwined with the right of happiness. As we are all given talents and abilities, we can use these to worship God and to acquire the property we desire. Ownership comes with the responsibility to enhance our belongings, to live our lives to serving God, and to be good stewards over our possessions. To beautify, to enhance, to enrich, and to share both our property and our lives will truly bring us happiness. Along life's journey, the pursuit thereof may be filled with thorns, rocks, and other obstacles, but in the end true happiness comes when we dedicate and consecrate our lives to Christian service. We've all heard, "You can't take it with you," meaning all material possessions, but what we can take with us is our devotion to serving the Lord Jesus Christ. Then he will provide us with all that our heavenly father has.

Example 1: William Blackstone, an English jurist, was the source for many of the laws developed by the founding fathers. His commentaries became a great resource on the role and purpose of just government.

Example 2: Alexis de Tocqueville understood the real meaning of democracy in America and the profound effect it had on American culture and success.

Scriptures: John 8:32; Galatians 2:4; 2 Nephi 2:27; Mosiah 2:41; John 13:17

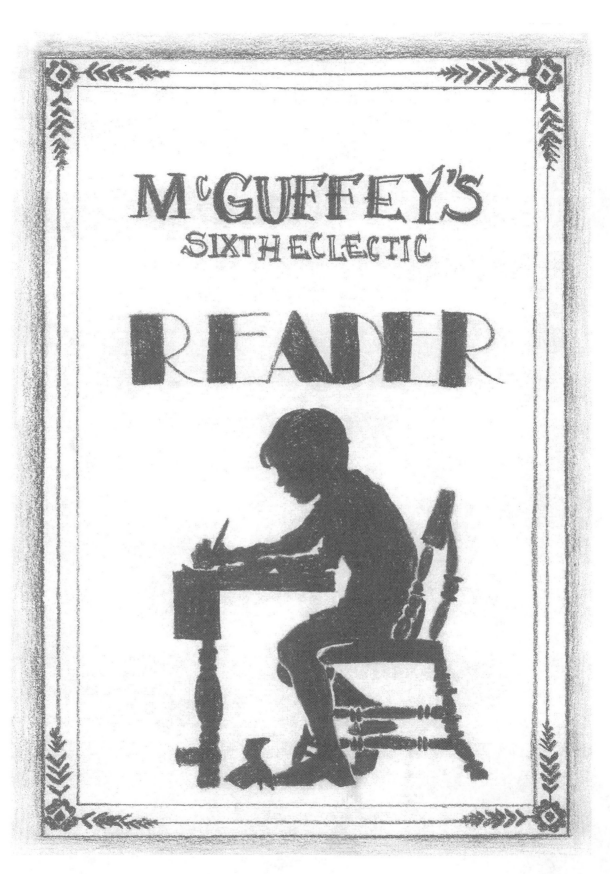

Chapter 9

McGuffey's Readers

The Christian Religion is a religion of our country. From it are derived our prevalent notions of the character of God, the great moral Governor of the universe. On its doctrines are founded the peculiarities of our free institutions.

—Reverend William Holmes McGuffey

In the 1830s, a minister by the name of William Holmes McGuffey started preparing a series of schoolbooks aimed at teaching students to read. Because of his Calvinist background, the lessons taught had a moral overtone and came from numerous sources. These eclectic readers quoted from many famous authors. These books had a tremendous influence on the educational mores of America and many are still in use to this day. At that time, one of the purposes of educating children was to pass on the idea of good citizenship while influencing the moral and cultural values of society.

I will begin by showing some examples from the readers themselves, and then I will make the transition to education in America, from the time of its founding up to the present day.

In the second eclectic reader, there's a story called "God is Great and Good."

1. I know God made the sun
To fill the day with light;
He made the twinkling stars
To shine all through the night.
2. He made the hills that rise
So very high and steep;
He made the lakes and seas
That are so broad and deep.
3. He made the streams so wide

That flow through wood and vale;
He made the rills so small
That leap down hill and dale.
4. He made each bird that sings
So sweetly all the day;
He made each flower that springs
So bright, so fresh, so gay.
5. And He who made all these,
He made both you and me;
Oh, let us thank him, then,
For great and good is He.

You can see from this excerpt how the author incorporated his Christian beliefs into the story so that children could be exposed to these beliefs.

Here's a synopsis of the story from the second reader. It is called "A Good Old Man."

A Good Old Man

There once lived an old man in a snug little cottage. It had two rooms and only two windows. A small garden lay just behind it. Old as the poor man was, he used to work in the fields. Often he would come home very tired and weak, with his hoe or spade on his shoulder. His two granddaughters would visit on occasion, but they were too small to work in the garden. They would sit on their grandfather's knee as he told them stories or taught them. The girls' father had gone out to sea, and they anxiously awaited his return. The old man got weaker year by year, and as they got older, the girls were glad to do some work for him. On one cold and windy night, their father came home from his travels on the sea. He had saved some money, and now he was going to stay home. After his son's arrival, the old man did not have to work hard anymore. His son worked for him, and the granddaughters helped take care of their grandfather as their mother was gone. They spent many happy days together.

As you examine each of the readers, you will find countless examples of moral underpinnings associated with the poems and stories that fill the pages. These days we have forgotten the value of teaching moral concepts to our children. Let us turn our attention to the general discourse of education in America.

A phrase from the Northwest Ordinance (passed in 1787 for the governance of territory northwest of the Ohio River) instructed that religion, morality, and knowledge being necessary to good government and the happiness of mankind, schools and a means of education should forever be encouraged.

John Adams stated, "Children should be educated and instructed in the principles of freedom."

Another quote, from Noah Webster, stated, "It is an object of vast magnitude that systems of education should be adopted and pursued which may not only diffuse a knowledge of the sciences but may implant in the minds of the American youth the principles of virtue and of liberty and inspire them with just and liberal ideas of government and with an inviolable attachment to their own country."

We begin with a look at the New England primer, the first established curriculum that taught not only reading but also Christian character. It included little tidbits that taught the alphabet with Christian themes. An example for the letters is as follows: "In Adam's fall we sinned all; Thy life to mend, God's book attend; Queen Esther comes in Royal state, to save the Jews from dismal fate; and Time cuts down all, both great and small." The primer also included the Lord's Prayer, certain creeds, a morning and evening prayer, the golden rule, life-and-death questions, the Ten Commandments, verses for little children, and a short version of the catechism. So intertwined was the teaching of reading and writing with the moral discourse on Christian behavior that it provided a sound framework for those who experienced this instruction. We also note that some parents had their children tutored at home or had clergyman take in students as borders and mentor them in preparation for going to college. Sometimes male students would serve as apprentices to craftsmen or someone skilled in a trade, taking up to seven years to become experienced. Both males and females were taught not only English but also Latin.

As for colleges, the first four established in America were really Christian seminaries. Their desire to teach the students to know God and Jesus Christ as a foundation for all other knowledge and learning was the main purpose for the schools. Harvard was established in Boston when John Harvard left over four hundred books from his library in order to create a seminary for inquiring students. There was a distinct correlation between theology and government. Many of the founding fathers were taught from theological textbooks. One can look at the laws and statutes that each student had to read and agree to for examples of the fusion between theological instruction and Christian behavior.

The College of William and Mary was established in 1693 in Virginia. It instructed the students in the common law of England, and each had to swear allegiance to Almighty God. As they studied political philosophy and legal education, it provided a sound basis for the upcoming revolution.

Yale University was founded in 1701 in New Haven, Connecticut, by a group of ministers, and it provided an alternative to Harvard University. The education developed here provided the seeds for many of the revolutionaries who would eventually help form the establishment of America.

Princeton University was founded by the Presbyterian synod as a place where students could come without having to travel out of state to other colleges. As with the other schools, Princeton was established to promote and advance Christianity. The school had a tremendous effect on the patriots who were instrumental in establishing the American government.

We will turn our thoughts now to the concept of classical education, which has its history dating back to the ancient Romans and Greeks. The term *liberal education* came from the Latin word *libera*, which means free. In the Middle Ages, educators developed a liberal education comprised of the seven liberal arts. It consisted of two parts, the first of which was the *trivium* of grammar, logic, and rhetoric. The second part, called the *quadrivium*, consisted of mathematics, music, astronomy, and geometry. The students who were educated in the seven arts went on to study the physical sciences, natural science, history, politics, law, and theological science. From here the students could go into the professions of law or medicine or they could choose the church. This educational process helped the student gain mastery in each subject by teaching them basic facts, the ability to be creative, and the skills to communicate ideas clearly and effectively. This would be a formidable education for any student.

There developed also an educational philosophy called *Christian classicism*. This was for the purpose of not only educating children in the arts and sciences but also continuing to build their faith by teaching the principles found in the Bible. Over the years there have been many models of classical education. In our day there has been an ever-increasing homeschooling movement; many of these use the principles of classical education intertwined with the moral teachings of the Christian faith.

Although there are a few good religious schools in the country, most of the major universities have a far different approach to education. Not only is religion removed from the curriculum, it is replaced by what one might call *liberal socialism*. It seems that through the centuries there have always been men who think their philosophy is far more important than that of God. As we have been lax in the promotion of Christian ideals and values, we have seen an ever-increasing emphasis on secular thought and ideas.

We can agree that in preparation for college, the academic subjects of English, the arts, mathematics, science, social studies, foreign language, and computer skills and competency are important. Many schools have watered down the curriculum and have inflated grades and test scores. The graduation rate at many high schools is alarming, and we find that many of those who do graduate are not prepared for college. We have abandoned rigor and relevance in our studies and have failed, in many cases, to emphasize critical thinking and problem-solving. Who cannot agree that the abandonment of Christian ideals has had a profound effect on the education of our children? Either we are a Christian nation or not. If we are, then the practice of moral decision-making is of the utmost importance. It was C. S. Lewis who said, "We all want progress, but if you're on the wrong road, progress means doing an about turn and walking back to the right road; in that case, the man who turns back soonest is the most progressive." Many people have felt that we are on the wrong road as a nation, for the modern idea of progressivism means that we are depending upon the government for most of our needs instead of relying on ourselves with a firm conviction of biblical principles and teachings. Finally, C. S. Lewis warned, "The safest road to hell is a gradual one—the gentle slope, soft underfoot, without sudden turnings, without milestones, without signposts." We must be careful not to put our trust and faith in a corrupt and evil world. Our government has begun to lead us down this gradual slope by denying the people the right to be taught not only in academics but in Christian ideals, which was the bedrock of the founding of our great country.

Example 1: C. S. Lewis was a great teacher and writer of Christian values and morals. His complete works are a must for any serious student engaged in the education of moral decision-making.

Example 2: Neal A Maxwell was a professor at the University of Utah who later became an apostle for the Church of Jesus Christ of Latter-day Saints. His teaching style and knowledge of both academic and spiritual concepts made him a great example of a master teacher.

Scriptures: Proverbs 1:5; John 5:39; Alma 37:8; Doctrine and Covenants 88:118; 2 Timothy 3:16

Chapter 10

POOR RICHARD'S ALMANACK

No man can be happy without virtue.

—Benjamin Franklin

Benjamin Franklin published his series of almanacs between the years 1733 and 1758. They were very popular among the colonists and had a great influence on colonial life. They consisted of verses along with observations of a historical nature and of the scientific world. They also included rules of health, Proverbs, and ideas on how to be rich. He included the wisdom of the ages and borrowed some themes from Dryden, Pope, and Rabelais. His adages and sayings became a part of everyday speech, being used in sermons, mottos, and pamphlets and newspapers. We will examine some of his writings with the intent of finding a moral meaning buried deep within the content of his publication.

"He that lies down with dogs shall rise up with fleas." How appropriate is this saying that tells us that our decisions are very important? We cannot escape the consequences of our behavior.

"The heart of a fool is in his mouth, but the mouth of a wise man is in his heart." There is much to be said about the unkind words that emerge from the mouths of many people. With all of the argument, disparagement, accusations, and unsavory remarks, especially in the area of politics, we see a total disregard for anything civil.

"Where carcasses are, eagles will gather, and where the good laws are, much people flock thither." The founding fathers understood the relationship between good laws and helping protect the rights the people. They were also aware that it was even more important to follow God's laws.

"All things are easy to industry, all things difficult to sloth." He who is not willing to work to reap the benefits of his labor should not expect that anyone else, including the government, should help him along and enable him to be dependent.

"It is better to take many injuries than to give one." Christ taught us to love our neighbors and also our enemies. He was the one who took upon himself not only the sins of the world but all of the infirmities, pains, and sufferings that could be inflicted on us. He bore all the injuries that could plague the human condition. If we are to follow him, then we need to apply the moral decision to not be injurious to others.

"The noblest question in the world is, what good may I do in it?" There are many people around the world, especially those who live in Third-World countries, who don't have enough food and water to supply their needs. While we reap the benefits of our hard work, we have the opportunity to share with those less fortunate. There are many worthwhile charities and organizations whose sole purpose is to help alleviate human suffering. The Church of Jesus Christ of Latter-day Saints frequently send out from their storehouses supplies such as food, medicine, clothing, and other goods and services. It has thousands of volunteers who help people every day to get the basic needs of food, clothing, and shelter. The moral decision to help others in need is one of the basic tenets of Christianity.

"Think of three things: whence you came, where you are you going, and to whom you must account." Life on earth did not just start spontaneously. All of us lived as spirit children in heaven with God. He sent us here to learn to be obedient to His laws and commandments; in doing so, we can end up back where we started, in heaven with God. He requires of us, through his son Jesus Christ, to follow his example. We will be accountable to him for our actions and the way we live our lives.

"How many observe Christ's birthday, how few his precepts." In our day we have gotten to the point where it is not even legal to celebrate Christmas. Instead, we must call it a "holiday celebration." We have eliminated the manger scene, the Ten Commandments, and other religious symbols in the public arena. It becomes harder to observe and keep God's precepts because of the elimination of any Christian symbolism. I remember an anonymous quote I heard one time that went like this: "One is not what one says he is but what he demonstrates himself to be." There are many who say the right words at the right time, but their actions are far different from what they're saying. In politics, especially, it has become the norm for candidates to tell the people what they want to hear. They keep promising, they keep talking, but their policies do not help the people.

"Don't throw stones at your neighbors if your own windows are glass." When the Savior was dealing with the woman who was about to be stoned for the sin of adultery, he taught a powerful lesson. He told the accusers that whoever was without sin should cast the first stone. I'm sure that hit them like a ton of bricks, for they all would have realized that they were hypocrites. The Savior then told the woman that he would forgive her but that she should go and sin no more. It takes a lot of willpower to not cast the first stone.

"To God we owe fear and love; to our neighbors justice and charity; to ourselves prudence and sobriety." This is Christian living in a concise and clear example. As we contemplate our relationship with God, with our neighbors, and with ourselves, we are reminded of how we should act in each situation when dealing with these three entities.

These are just some of the tidbits of wisdom gathered from Franklin's writings. They are intended to help us on our journey through the world in which we live. There are many who would discount such counsel and advice and lean to the philosophies of men. But a Christian's life is much more rewarding and has an eternal meaning attached to it. May we use moral decisions in the way we govern ourselves and the way we react to others.

Example 1: Benjamin Franklin was an inventor, politician, and statesman who helped form this great nation.

Example 2: Thomas Jefferson was another key figure in the formation of America as a nation. He has been called the father of the Declaration of Independence.

Scriptures: Luke 2:51; John 8:51; Doctrine and Covenants 66:11; Philip 4:8; 2 Peter 1:5

Chapter 11

REFORMATION TO REVOLUTION
TO RESTORATION

I have sought nothing beyond reforming the church in conformity with the Holy Scriptures.

—Martin Luther

After the period known as the Dark Ages, some illumination came into the church when the people began to be able to read the Scriptures, which had been translated into Latin and then into English. In 1388 John Wycliffe completed the English translation of the Bible. There were many others who became involved in what is known as the Protestant Reformation. Let us examine a few of these people; they set the stage for events that would eventually lead to the discovery of America. John Wycliffe was a reformer who was critical of the Catholic Church; he was later tried as a heretic. Jan Hus was a bohemian reformer who was burned at the stake. Christopher Columbus made his first voyage to America in 1492. Martin Luther, the most prominent of the reformers, in 1517 nailed his ninety-five theses to the door of the Wittenberg Castle Church. William Tyndale published his English version of the Bible in Germany. After smuggling copies of the Bible into England, he was burned at the stake in 1536. John Calvin let the Reformation in Geneva, Switzerland, and John Knox established the Protestant religion in Scotland.

As we turn our attention to the settlement of America, we see that there were many historic events and people who helped develop them. This opened doors to the eventual colonization of this great land. In 1607, the first permanent English settlement was established in Jamestown. In 1620, the pilgrims founded what is known today as Massachusetts, at Plymouth. The Dutch settlers founded New Amsterdam, which was to become New York City. The Puritans founded the Massachusetts Bay colony. Roger Williams, an advocate for freedom of religion, founded Providence, Rhode Island. He was aided by Anne Hutchinson, after she was banished from Massachusetts.

William Penn, an English Quaker, settled Pennsylvania. After John Wesley started the Methodist movement in England, the Methodist Episcopal Church was organized in America. Ann Lee, founder of the Shaker movement in England, eventually came to America in 1774. We can see that as people had at their disposal the Bible, which they were now able to read, it became evident that the church that Christ had established was nothing like what was being offered by the Catholic Church at that time. The people experienced a great awakening, and with the discovery of America, they found a land that would be tolerant of their religious beliefs and allow them to worship according to the dictates of their own consciences.

The English Common Law, which was codified by King Alfred around 890 AD, was modified over the years and became the basis for the founding fathers to develop a constitutional government in America. These legal principles prohibited certain behaviors which were said to be offenses to God. The Judeo Christian morality was explicitly mentioned in this body of laws. Such behaviors as Sabbath-breaking, cursing, homosexuality, fornication and adultery, prostitution, gambling, and drunk and disorderly conduct were explicitly considered unlawful. Today, we have repealed many of these types of laws in the name of expediency and for being "too religious." What a grave mistake this has been, because it has allowed all sorts of behaviors, many of which defy Christian behavior, to be accepted and protected under current law. If we say to ourselves that we are not a Christian nation and that there is no room for God's law in our society, then we are slowly creeping toward Gomorrah.

The revolution in America was an extension of the Protestant Reformation that had occurred in Europe. That any people should be confined by a government that usurped their power was inconceivable, and freedom became the battle cry for independence from England. The abuses were magnified to the extent that people lost their freedom. We must understand that the founders understood that natural rights come from God and that all men have a right to live under a government that secures rights rather than taking them away. In Samuel Adams's Committees of Correspondence, he declared the rights of the colonists, saying, "Just and true liberty, equal and impartial liberty, in matters spiritual and temporal, is a thing that all men are entitled to by the eternal and immutable laws of God and nature, as well as by the law of nations and well-grounded municipal laws, which must have their foundation and the former …{These (rights) may be best understood by reading carefully and studying the institutes of the great lawgiver and head of the Christian church, which are found clearly written and promulgated in the New Testament."}

How did a far-inferior army overcome the great British Empire with its superior forces? This remains today the most puzzling of questions. When we study these events, we come to understand that God had a prophetic destiny for the establishment of America. Thomas Jefferson once said, "The religion builders have so distorted and deformed the doctrines of Jesus, so muffle them in mysticisms, fancies, and falsehoods, have caricatured them into forms so inconceivable, as a shock reasonable thinker". He also said," I must leave to younger Athletes to encounter to lop off the false branches which have been engrafted into it by the mythologists of the middle and modern ages."" Where else could these principles of freedom and religious rights be established but in this foreordained land of promise? Elder Bruce R. McConkie, one of the twelve apostles of the Church of Jesus Christ of Latter-day Saints, said in a 1974 conference report, "The work to be done by John the Baptist, by the ancient twelve, by Columbus, by the signers of the Declaration of Independence, and by the framers of the Constitution of the United States was all known and arranged far in advance. In all, these are but illustrations and patterns, for all the Lord's work is planned and prepared in advance, and those who are called and chosen to do the work receive their commission and ordination from him, first in the preexistence and then, if they remain true and faithful, again here in mortality." We can see that the power of God was with Columbus, the reformers, the colonists, and many others who helped shape the destiny of this great land.

After the Revolutionary war, there was a notion among many who wanted to make George Washington a king. He firmly resisted this idea by this statement: "With a mixture of great surprise and astonishment, I have read with attention the sentiment you have submitted to my perusal. Be assured, sir, no occurrence in the course of the war has given me more painful sensations than your information of there being such ideas existed in the Army as you have expressed, and I must view them with abhorrence and reprimand with severity. For the present communication they will rest in my own bosom, unless some further agitation of the matter shall make a disclosure necessary. I am much at a loss to conceive what part of my conduct good have given encouragement to an address, which to me seems big with the greatest mischiefs that can befall my country. If I am not deceived in the knowledge of myself, you could not have found a person to whom your schemes are more disagreeable. Let me assure you, then, if you have any regard for your country, concern for yourself or posterity, or respect for me, to banish these thoughts from your mind and never communicate, as from yourself or anyone else, a sentiment of the like nature."" This great leader understood that personal desires were to be directed at the formation of his country and not in any way at the desires of others who wanted him to be a king.

The Apostle Peter, in Acts 3, said, "He shall send Jesus Christ, the heaven must receive until the times of restitution of all things, which God has spoken by the mouth of all his holy prophets since the world began." We have explored the founding of

America and the establishment of religious freedom. God-given rights made it a land where the full gospel of Jesus Christ could be established.

According to Abraham Lincoln, "It is a duty of nations as well as of men to own their dependence upon the overruling power of God, to confess their sins and transgressions in humble sorrow, yet with a short hope that genuine repentance will lead to mercy and to recognize the sublime truth, announced in the holy Scriptures and proven by all history, that those nations only are blest whose God is the Lord.""

Roger Williams once said, "There is no regularly constituted church on earth, nor any person qualified to administer any church ordinances; nor can there be until new apostles are sent by the great head of the church whose coming I am seeking." The Church of Jesus Christ of Latter-day Saints firmly declares that when Joseph Smith organized the church in 1830, it was established once again as a church that had apostles and prophets.

We may wonder why the United States was chosen for the sacred restoration of the gospel of Jesus Christ. In this world, only a fraction of the people call themselves Christians. Many have not even heard of Jesus Christ but have been indoctrinated in the teachings of the more infamous communist rulers. Many people do not have sufficient food or clothing or other necessities of life. The United States has been blessed not only temporally but also spiritually and has been commissioned a leader to help ease the world of its burdens.

Out of obscurity came the boy Joseph Smith. What he accomplished in a short life span cannot be ignored or overlooked. He was a humble youth looking for an answer to a question he had about the many churches that were fervently preaching the gospel. Elder Dallin H. Oaks, of the quorum of the twelve apostles, said this about Joseph Smith: "Joseph was an incredible man. For someone to walk large on the stage of history and accomplish incredible things without a remarkable invention, or an inherited fortune, or a stroke of luck, or discovering something is incredible."

Dr. Gordon Wood, of Brown University, stated, "Joseph Smith is obviously the most successful American prophet that we've ever had. He established a religion that has not only lasted but flourished and grown to become the most powerful, uniquely American religion we've ever had."

Speaking about America during this time, Dr. Robert Remini, of the University of Illinois at Chicago, said, "I would call the Democratic Revolution a shorthand term for the awakening of ordinary folk, with a coming into consciousness of thousands upon thousands of ordinary people who up to that time had been simply not part of the historical record. They simply hadn't counted for anything, and all the sudden—I think this happens throughout the Western world but particularly in the United States—they come into their own. They find that they do count for something, that they matter, and there is a new sense of their power. And they bring with them into consciousness not only democracy as we understand it—popular democracy, popular politics—but they bring with them their religious consciousness, their religious feelings, and their emotions." He also went on the say about Joseph Smith, "Do I personally believe? No. He may have believed that he did. But whether he saw, I have no evidence for that. And as a historian, I must base my conclusion on that. Since I'm not a Mormon by an act of faith who believes it, even though it can be proved, I have to then make a judgment on the basis of the evidence. However, you can say, 'Look at what he did. Is one human being capable of doing this? Without divine help or intervention.'"

Finally, Dr. Nathan Hatch, of the University of Notre Dame, made this comment: "The fact that there were so many religious voices was very bewildering, I think, for common people. And so there was this deep questioning. What could one believe? And I think that's where the voice of Joseph Smith did become a very certain trumpet. What he said is that he had a new word from the Lord, a new kind of revelation, which was certain and sure. It was a miraculous intervention in modern times, just as Christ did in the time of the New Testament. And that makes great sense to a lot of people, that amidst this cacophony of voices you had a certain trumpet that offered the reality of the supernatural today."

Joseph Smith established the Church of Christ, translated from ancient records the book of Mormon, published his revelations, and offered a new way of life to his followers. He died a martyr, but his spirit still lives on in the hearts and minds of millions of his followers. Be sure that this was not the church of Joseph Smith but the church of Christ, he being the cornerstone of that religion.

Example 1: William Tyndale was a reformer who was martyred for his faith. He translated the bible. He described his faith as a "fire in the bones."

Example 2: Joseph Smith was a prophet and organizer of the Church of Jesus Christ of Latter-day Saints. He was also martyred for his faith and devotion to God. He also translated from ancient records, the book of Mormon.

Scriptures: Isaiah 2:2; Matthew 17:11; Abraham 2:19; Articles of Faith 10

Chapter 12

SEEDS AND THE SOWER

Anyone can count the seeds in an apple, but only God can count the number of apples in a seed.

—Robert H. Schuller

Ever since God created the Garden of Eden, placed Adam and Eve there, and gave them the fruit and herbs to eat, seeds have played a major role in the formation of the earth to distribute beauty and nourishment to all mankind. We are going to look at seeds from two different perspectives: one aspect will be the physical seeds that are planted to start the process of growth, and the second aspect will be a spiritual point of view, the way in which the master sower taught his precepts in parables and other story forms.

In ancient times, the Hanging Gardens of Babylon were spectacular; they have been declared one of the seven wonders of the ancient world. All across the globe we can see the loveliness of plants, flowers, fruits, trees, herbs, and other forms of vegetation. They give beauty to this wonderful world in which we live. On a personal level, many of us, me included, have planted gardens where we can harvest the fruits of our labors. There is something unique about working the soil, planting some seeds, watering, weeding, fertilizing, and finally enjoying the harvest. I live in a farming community in southeastern Idaho, where the crops of potatoes, grains, hay, and other commodities are planted and harvested for capital gain. Growing up working on my uncle's farm, tending to the cows and other livestock, and hauling in the hay by hand, I had generated in me a love for raising animals and working the soil.

If we start in the northeastern part of the United States and work our way across the continent from the Atlantic to the Pacific Ocean, we can see the magnificent display of flora that is found in our land. In the Appalachian Mountains we find both hardwood and softwood forests, including pines, maples, birch, oak, hickory, beach, fir, cedar, and other types of shrubs and flowers. Going south, we run into the cherry blossoms, the cypress swamps, trees covered with Spanish moss, and a whole array of beautiful flowers. In the Adirondack Mountains of upper New York State, the mostly wooded area offers breathtaking scenes of nature's beauty. In this area and in New England, who could help but feel awe and wonder at the magnificent fall display of changing colors? When we lived in New England, my wife and I gained a great feeling for the beauty of that area. After getting married, we purchased a small farm in Maine, where we raised livestock, had a large garden, made maple syrup from the trees on our property, and enjoyed the beautiful landscape of both the interior and coastal regions of this place.

As we crisscross the American continent, we come across such areas as America's heartland, the dairy land, the land of the Ozarks, bayou country, the magnificent Rockies, the Great Plains, the Grand Canyon, the redwood forests, and beautiful national parks. We enjoy a host of plants, birds, and animals in each of these areas.

In Genesis 1:11–12 we read, "And God said, let the earth bring forth grass, the herb yielding seed, and the fruit tree yielding fruit after its kind, and the tree yielding fruit, whose seed within itself, after his kind: and God saw that it was good. And the earth brought forth grass, the herb yielding seed after his kind, and the tree yielding fruit, whose seed was in itself, after his kind: and God saw that it was good." Once we acknowledge that God the Father and his son, Jesus Christ, were the creators of this world, and once we recognize the beauty that surrounds us, we will be more appreciative of its magnificence.

Since the beginning of time, sowing seeds to produce the food needed for the sustenance of every human has been at best a futile effort; there are millions who day after day face hunger and even starvation. In the days of Moses, when the people of Israel were roaming through the desert, the Lord provided manna for them to eat. In Exodus 16:31 we read the following: "And the house of Israel called the name thereof manna: and it was like coriander seed, white; and the taste of it was like wafers made with honey." The Lord has said that there are more than enough resources to meet the necessities for all people. The problem today is one of distribution and also the greed and avarice of those leaders who would use those resources as a club over the people, not allowing them to even have the basic necessities of life. In order for people to accept gospel principles, they must first have these physical needs met.

The Church of Jesus Christ of Latter-day Saints has aided in the relief for millions of people around the world, with such services as wheelchair distribution, vision treatment, natural-disaster relief, measles vaccination, and clean-water projects. Through other organizations, they have donated both time and money. It is our God-given responsibility to help comfort those in need, regardless of who they are and what they may have done. We should read the story of the Good Samaritan and remember that all of God's children are our neighbors. We who have so much are required to share, and when we do, it becomes an act of love and brings joy to our hearts, our minds, and our souls.

In the book of Matthew, Jesus gave the parable of the man who went out to sow some seeds. In this parable, we begin to look at seeds from a religious point of view. Some of the seeds fell by the wayside, where the Savior said the flies came and devoured them. By the wayside, where there was no soil or dirt in which the seed could grow, the seeds were easy pickings for the fowl to come and pluck up. The fowl are people who are swayed by every whim and notion that comes their way; they lack any solid belief system.

The next seeds fell on some rocky places with a little soil. They sprouted, but because they lacked the depth needed to anchor down, as soon as the sun beat down its rays, they shriveled up and died due to lack of endurance. You've heard people who say, "I have a half a mind to do this or that" but are shallow in their thoughts and actions.

Some of the seeds fell among thorns, where they were not able to survive and were choked out because of lack of care. There are thorns that spring up all around us in our pathways through life, and if we are not careful, they can choke any belief or standard that we are trying to live by. We need to practice moral decision-making to be able to withstand our adversaries' attempts to squeeze the decency and honor out of us.

The last of the seeds fell on good ground, and they managed to grow and to magnify themselves. It is interesting to note that some of the seeds were more prosperous and brought forth more fruit than some of the others. We know that each of us has talents and abilities, but these are not all of the same capacity. Therefore, we make do with what we have and concentrate on our efforts to be the best we can be. There may be others who outperform us in various ways; the Bible says that where much is given much is expected. Nevertheless, each of us can grow to fruition on the good ground of the gospel. Eric Burdon, the musician, once said, "Inside each of us, there is a seed of both good and evil. It's a constant struggle as to which one will win. And one cannot exist without the other." This battle can be won as we dedicate our lives to Jesus Christ.

Ellen G. White, a Seventh-Day Adventist said, "Talk unbelief, you will have unbelief; but talk faith, and you will have faith. According to the seed sown will be the harvest." It is our hope that we will generate faith in God and not in the philosophies of men.

William Shakespeare said, "We cannot conceive of matter being formed of nothing, since things require a seed to start from … Therefore there is not anything which returns to nothing, but all things return dissolved into their elements."

We know that every human consists of a body in the spirit and that spirit and body will be reunited in the glorious hereafter. We have within us the seeds of deity and if faithful we can return to that God who is the father of our spirits. This kind of faith and hope requires time, patience, and sometimes a lifetime to recognize. But eventually we will see the fruits of our labor, as eloquently put by Mamata Banerjee: "Change is a continuous process. You cannot assess it with the static yardstick of a limited time frame. When a seed is sown into the ground, you cannot immediately see the plan. You have to be patient. With time it grows into a large tree. And then the flowers bloom, and only then can the fruits be plucked." Our challenge is to start now to do the best we can to sow the seeds on good ground, not only for our own benefit but for the benefit of others who come into our lives.

Example 1: Jesus Christ was the ultimate sower of good seeds. His gospel leads to an abundant life wherein we can live again, with Him and our Father, in heaven.

Example 2: The Apostle Peter became the leader of the church after the death of Christ and became a stalwart defender of the faith. He, with the other apostles, built the church around the world.

Scriptures: Matthew 13:4–7; Luke 8:11; Ecclesiasts 11:5; Psalm 19

Chapter 13

A TIME FOR CHOOSING

And this idea that government is beholden to the people, that it has no other source of power except the sovereign people, is still the newest and most unique idea in all the long history of man's relation to man.

—Ronald Reagan

"A Time for Choosing" was the title of a speech Ronald Reagan gave as they were nominating Barry Goldwater for the Republican presidential candidate. Although Goldwater was defeated by Lyndon Johnson, this was the start of the conservative movement that culminated later on in the election of Reagan as president for two terms. Let us examine the highlights of this speech and see if there is a correlation between that time and our present time in relation to the influence of government over the people.

The first of the complaints against the government, according to Mr. Reagan, was the tax structure. He said, "No nation in history has ever survived a tax burden that reached a third of its national income." Today that burden is even greater because of the tremendous national debt we have incurred. It seems that the more revenues the government acquires, the more it spends, again and again. Each congressman has his own method of adding pork-barrel spending to the national debt.

Thomas Jefferson once wrote, "To take from one, because it is thought his own industry and that of his father's has acquired too much, in order to spare to others, who, or whose fathers, have not exercised equal industry and skill, is to violate arbitrarily the first principle of association, the guarantee to everyone the free exercise of his industry and the fruits acquired by it." The old adage that to rob Peter to pay Paul is true in our day with all of the social programs aimed at the redistribution of wealth.

In his classic book *The Wealth of Nations*, Adam Smith wrote, "There is no art which one government sooner learns of another than that of draining money from the pockets of the people." He went on to say, "The tax which each individual is bound to pay ought to be certain and not arbitrary. The time of payment, the manner of payment, the quantity to be paid, ought all to be clear and plain to the contributor, and to every other person." The redistribution of wealth seems to be the goal of the socialist movement in our country, and if not controlled will be the downfall of the free-market system, which has been the basis for the success of America.

Finally, Aristotle had this advice: "To give away money is an easy matter and in any man's power. But to decide to whom to give it, and how large and when, and for what purpose and how, is neither in every man's power or an easy matter." Most of us have to live within a budget with restraints on how much we spend while we try to avoid major debt. The government, on the other hand, does not treat the revenues it receives as a sacred trust from the people. Rather, it spends such revenues in an arbitrary and capricious manner, justifying its actions by extolling social programs which enable some to benefit from the work of others.

Mr. Reagan went on to talk about war as we had just become more involved in Vietnam. Peace and prosperity are elusive endeavors in a world that is being run largely by communist or socialist dictators. We should have learned our lessons from the Vietnam War. I was personally involved there, and I lost my right arm. But I came to love the Vietnamese people, many of whom were living in squalid conditions. I believe it was Johnson's idea that we could just bomb the North Vietnamese into submission. This proved to be a fatal error. In our day we have been involved in the Gulf War and wars in Afghanistan and Iraq. None of these endeavors has really created a lasting peace. We withdrew from Iraq but are now involved in Syria, in the whole Middle East. The government has not shown a real commitment to any kind of a foreign policy that will serve to end this conflict. The rise of the Taliban, Al Qaeda, and now Isis have stretched the global war on terror to unprecedented capacity. George Washington once said, "To be prepared for war is one of the most effectual means of preserving peace."

Alexander Hamilton, in his essay "Federalist No. 34," made this observation: "To judge from the history of mankind, we shall be compelled to conclude that the fiery and destructive passions of war reign in the human breast with much more powerful sway than the mild and beneficent sentiments of peace, and that to model our political systems upon speculations outlasting tranquility would be to calculate on the weaker springs of human character." Of course, no one wants war, but there are evil forces around the globe that glory in these conflicts. We must be ready and willing to upgrade our military forces so we are ready to engage the enemy wherever he may be.

When Reagan talked about limited government, he was referring to the concept that the American Revolution was fought over. The idea that any government can control the people's lives better than they can themselves is the predominant theme of liberalism. The founding fathers instituted a certain level of rights for the government.

These are things that they can do, but far too often they have expanded way beyond these enumerated duties to gain control over almost every aspect of our lives.

Lyndon Johnson ushered in what he called the Great Society, in which the federal government would have a greater influence in the affairs of the people. He believed that the free economic system, in which people through hard work earn a profit with which to pursue their own course of happiness, was outdated. He felt it should be replaced by the welfare system, which allows people to have the government solve their problems.

The individual who is responsible, while raising a family, should read to the words of Adam Smith when he said, "It is the maxim of every prudent master of a family never to attempt to make at home what it will cost him more to make than to buy. What is prudence in the conduct of every private family can scarcely be folly in that of a great kingdom." These principles outline what the founding fathers had in mind as guidelines of the great governmental system they produced. It will take hard moral decisions on the part of the people to bring us back to those standards that Ronald Reagan talked about in his speech.

Mr. Reagan then went on to talk about our relationship with countries around the world. He said, "I think we're for aiding our allies by sharing our material blessings with those nations which share in our fundamental beliefs, but we're against doling out money government to government, creating bureaucracy, if not socialism, around the world. We set out to help 19 countries. We're helping 107 … In the last six years, 52 nations have bought $7 million worth of our gold, and all 52 are receiving foreign aid from this country. We have been involved in the failed policy of trying to set up democracies all around the world. Even today, we have turned over billions of dollars to our sworn enemy, the Ayatollah of Iran—this under the guise of a nuclear deal. Our leadership, coming from behind, has created chaos and uncertainty all around the world. We have lost something—maybe it's respect, honor, or a willingness to lead—but it is lost in the entanglement of a foreign policy with no clear and sustainable goals."

George Washington once said, "'Tis our true policy to steer clear of permanent alliances, with any portion of the foreign world.

Thomas Jefferson added, "Peace, commerce, and honest friendship with all nations, entangling alliances with none. … We are firmly convinced, and we act on that conviction, that with nations as with individuals our interests soundly calculated will ever be found inseparable from our moral duties." There is no such thing as moral relativism, but rather, a firm conviction in the Christian morals that our founding fathers used to establish this great nation, are clearly defined in the Scriptures.

We, too, live in a time when we have to make a choice. There has been a moral decline not only in thought but also in behavior. We have seen the redefinition of marriage, an increase in crime void of any moral consequence, the emergence of a large monolithic government incapable of monitoring itself but affecting the lives of all people in a most negative way, the creation of a society in which people rely on the government instead of their own resources, and the lack of civility, which we touched on before, in human discourse and action.

We must ask ourselves questions about issues that confront us in our world today. Do we believe that human life is sacred and abortion comes very close to an act of murder? There are those who argue against the death penalty, calling it cruel and unjust punishment. But in the case of those who commit unspeakable crimes, it becomes a way of dealing with those who commit murder and other heinous crimes. Do we want the government to regulate our economy? Or should we leave it as is, with a free-market system that creates a high standard of living for all who participate with hard work and use their skills and talents to better their lives? Public education has become an enigma, with the elimination of prayer in the classroom, celebration of holidays instead of Christmas, and the reduction of anything of a spiritual nature. Hence we see an increasing number of parents who homeschool their children or use a voucher system to select the school they wish to send their children to. I have been a public educator all my life, and I have seen the results of a government-run school system that eliminates the teaching of a Christian values system. Do we want to have the opportunity to create our own independence for oil, natural gas, coal, and other resources, to eliminate our need of foreign sources?

I believe one of the most unscientific hoaxes pressed upon the American people and the world is that of global warming. Of course temperatures have fluctuated since the beginning of time. If we believe that God created this world with enough resources to sustain an even larger population, then it is hard to understand the reasoning of many on the left who say that we have overpopulation.

We have seen the results of a government-run health-care system, with its increases in premiums and the cancellation of many of the states' attempts, to conform to the law. We should have a privatized health-care system that people can access, and the ability to transfer it state to state, wherever they go. We do not want a government bureaucracy to determine which doctors we see and what care is available to us.

Immigration has become a hot topic once again. We agree that legal immigration is good for our country. There is a process whereby individuals can come and eventually earn the right to become citizens. It's interesting that the media refuses to call those who come illegally to our nation anything other than undocumented workers. If someone breaks a law, they must pay a penalty. We may not catch all the illegal immigrants here (neither do we catch all the people who have robbed banks), but those we do catch will be subject to the law. We have to protect our borders more efficiently, especially with the rise of global terrorists who can sneak through and enter almost any country at will.

These and other issues—such as private property, religion and government, same-sex marriage, welfare, taxes (which we touched on a little), and the war on terror—all require, not only for our leaders but for ourselves, some common-sense moral decision-making to deal with problems that have an eternal effect on our lives. Either we are a Christian nation or we're not. Either we have a moral value standard based on Christian ethics or not. Either we apply Christian values to our decision-making or we don't. The rewards of complying and the consequences of disobeying are at the root of our existence. We need leaders who exhibit high moral standards, decency, and respect for our country and for the Christian beliefs upon which it was founded.

Example 1: Ronald Reagan became a two-term president of the United States and exemplified how a true conservative government can operate and put the people first.

Example 2: Newt Gingrich, who worked with Reagan and became Speaker of the House, helped create a balanced budget and ushered in an era of sound economic growth.

Scriptures: Mosiah 2: 17; Doctrine and Covenants 4:2; Ephesians 6:7; Matthew 19:21; 2 Corinthians 8:5.

Chapter 14

VOLUNTEERISM

Service is never a simple act; it's about sacrifice for others and about accomplishment, about reaching out, one person to another, about all our choices gathered together as a country to reach across all our divides.

—George W. Bush

As a part of the American value system, volunteerism has played an integral role in shaping the goodness of this country's morality.

Clarence B. Carson once said, "Volunteerism is the means of undertaking joint ventures without the use of compulsion. It is a way of persuasion, not coercion; of choice, not dictation; of willed action, not forced participation; a variety, not uniformity; of competition, not monopoly of freedom, not subjection ... Volunteerism is a complementary side of the coin to individualism; it is a means of getting social tasks done that is consonant with liberty." There was a time in America when church attendance was mandated; well, compulsory education had not yet been established. It should be remembered that one of the drawing cards to the American continent was freedom of religion. Church attendance embodied the idea of morality and good citizenship. Since the first established settlement at Jamestown—which in and of itself was an act of volunteerism on the part of the people—and the arrival of the Mayflower, whose passengers formed a pact to help each other in this new land, the idea of shared help took root. It was understood at the time of the revolution that there would be volunteers needed to help fight for freedom.

The colonists banded together to help face the realities of the harsh new world to which they had come. They worked together to plant crops and build their houses, and they provided help for those who became sick. We hear also of many who volunteered as firefighters and aided in the boycott of British goods coming into America.

During the Civil War years, such organizations as Ladies' Aid Societies sprang up to help with the war effort. Other examples of voluntary groups include, but are certainly not limited to, the New England barn-raising cooperative, clubs like Rotary, Kiwanis, and Lions, which all sprang up as nonprofit groups. Farmers got together and established ranges. During the Great Depression the government set up the organization called Volunteers of America. Of course, many church and civic groups have always been involved in helping ease people's burdens, not only in America but around the world. The idea of men and women getting together to pool their resources for such services as law and order, schooling, hospital services, and orphanages resulted in a provision of these services that otherwise would not have been available.

President Franklin Pierce, in declining the use of the federal government in providing services to its people, said this: "I readily, and I trust feelingly, acknowledge the duty incumbent on all of us, as men and citizens, and as among the highest and holiest of our duties, to provide for those who, in the mysterious order of Providence, are subject to want and to disease of body or mind, but I cannot find any authority in the Constitution for making the federal government the great almoner of public charity throughout the United States … It would, in the end, be prejudicial rather than beneficial to the noble offices of charity."

Toward the end of the nineteenth century, and well into our present time, there have been the unavoidable consequences of shifting from volunteerism to the idea of compulsory federal government dictates. As state and federal governments have become larger and more intricate, the tendency has been for them to solve issues that would be better left to the volunteer spirit of the citizens. Through the use of executive orders, a liberal court view, and certain legislation, we have abandoned the best way of solving social and economic problems, which is the art of volunteerism.

Let us review some ideas about volunteerism and examine the many facets of how this work continues in our day. Mother Teresa said, "There is a tremendous strength that is going in the world through … sharing together, praying together, suffering together, and working together." She went on to say: "Let us not be satisfied with just giving money. Money is not enough; money can be got, but they need your hearts to love them. So, spread your love everywhere you go."

Dr. Martin Luther King said this: "We are prone to judge success by the index of our salaries or the size of our automobiles rather than by the quality of our service relationship to humanity."

Finally, here's one more quote, from Lao Tzu: "Learn to lead in a nourishing manner. Learn to lead without being possessive. Learn to be helpful without taking the credit. Learn to lead without coercion."

We all understand that the government has its role in protecting the rights of its citizens. But as it becomes more and more monolithic, it takes the resources of the people and tries to redistribute them in a most pernicious way, in order to feed this growing, cumbersome entity. Thankfully there are many individuals and groups that continue to volunteer of their time, talents, and resources to help ease the pain and suffering of all peoples around the world.

I'll discuss one of these organizations with which I am familiar. The Church of Jesus Christ of Latter-day Saints, commonly known as the Mormons, are exemplary in the use of volunteers. There was a study done at the University of Pennsylvania by professor Ram Cnaan and researchers Van Evans and Daniel W. Curtis, which they published. It was titled "Called to Serve: The Prosocial Behavior of Active Latter-day Saints."

Some of the data provided revealed that the average American donates about 48 hours a year, while an active latter-day saint volunteers about 427 hours annually—which is worth about $9140. There is no paid clergy in the LDS church, and all auxiliaries are filled by volunteers. Latter-day saints also dedicate about 150 hours annually to such programs as the Boy Scouts or humanitarian-aid programs. Charitable donations include a 10 percent tithe on income, fast offerings, missionary funds, and humanitarian aid.

The church also participates in assisting families throughout the world by distributing food, medical supplies, and other resources. The church maintains and operates bishops' storehouses, where people can receive food commodities. They are also involved in family-counseling services, food-production facilities, and employment centers. They respond to disasters wherever they occur around the world. They have donated to the immunization of children and newborn care, have donated wheelchairs and glasses, and help supervise clean-water initiatives. They also partner with governments, other organizations such as the Red Cross, and Catholic charities, as well as businesses and other groups.

You might ask, why is this so important? The resources that come into the church are considered sacred and are not to be mishandled in any way. The ability to use these resources in the most constructive way is the epitome of moral decision-making. Imagine that the federal government were to operate with this kind of system—what a benefit it would be to its citizens! But we know that in such a large government system there is much fraud, waste, skimming off the top, and mismanagement of funds. This happens not only here but even more so in dictatorial governments around the world, where the people who are in need of the resources to sustain their lives go unserved and suffer greatly because nobody is allocating those resources in an honest and efficient manner.

As for individuals, there are many choices we can make in order to help alleviate pain and suffering right in our own communities, across the state, across the nation, and around the world. We are, for all intents and purposes, people who believe in philanthropy. We give of our time, talents, and resources, and we especially offer spiritual as well as temporal aid.

The command that the Savior gave in the Scriptures was to first love God and then to love our neighbors as ourselves. In this modern-day culture of entitlement, many people depend on the government for basically all of their needs. The redistribution of resources is hardly helpful in making people responsible for their own decisions. People are always willing to help one another, but there comes a time when the individual must take personal responsibility for his or her actions. Wrong decisions made at the moral, economic, or social level have their consequences. Of course we are morally obligated to help anyone, provided they take the initiative to shoulder some of the responsibility. God himself has said that he will not force anyone into heaven. So we teach, cajole, forgive, and love the people we come in contact with. The Church of Jesus Christ of Latter-day Saints has about eighty thousand missionaries around the world. As well, there are hundreds of thousands of volunteers who offer Christ-like service to those in need. We take care of the physical needs of the people and then offer them the hope that the gospel of Jesus Christ can bring to their lives. We applaud all Christian groups and charitable organizations who, likewise, are sharing of their abundance to help the needs of the poor. Volunteerism is alive and well in America.

Obviously, it takes not only physical courage but also moral courage to do our part in volunteering our lives in different ventures. Moral decision-making requires us to do good to any and all of God's children. As we forget our own problems and concentrate on the far-worse problems of others, there is much we can do. There is an endless list of things that even the elderly or homebound or physically disabled can accomplish. It has been my strategy while serving as a therapist to always try to get my clients involved in some kind of group activity. For the veterans, it was being involved in one of the service organizations. For students at school, it was to perform some service to those in the community who were in need. For my own children, it was to reach out to others, especially at certain holiday seasons throughout the year.

We should give special recognition to the men and women of the armed services who are faithfully serving their country in faraway places with strange-sounding names. For the families of those who have fallen in this great duty, and to those who suffer the physical and emotional wounds of war, we especially honor and remember them. No greater love can anyone display than in laying down his or her life for another. This biblical injunction carries with it the hope and promise of eternal life. May we always remember that volunteerism, in any capacity, is our gift to our father in heaven and his son, Jesus Christ. We will grow more as a people and as a nation when we follow the teachings that are found in the Scriptures.

To all who offer their services as volunteers, we commend you and thank you for your dedicated service. We know that you have made honorable moral decisions in your efforts. May God bless each of you, and may God bless America.

Example 1: All of the nonprofit organizations that exist to help alleviate world problems such as food and water shortage, disaster relief, and the need for medical supplies.

Example 2: Every individual who donates his or her time, talents, and resources to help give needed relief to people locally, nationally, and worldwide.

Scriptures: Mosiah 2: 17; Doctrine and Covenants 4:2; Ephesians 6:7; Matthew 19:21; 2 Corinthians 8:5

Chapter 15

THE WIZARD OF OZ

No matter how dreary and gray our homes are, we people of flesh and blood would rather live there than any other country, be it ever so beautiful. There is no place like home.

—Dorothy, in L. Frank Baum's story *The Wizard of Oz*

How many of us were delighted and sometimes a little scared watching the show *The Wizard of Oz*? I know my children were afraid of the flying monkeys and the wicked witch. What a wonderful delight that movie was and still is; it has touched the hearts of millions. In the town where I lived several years ago, we put on this play as a community endeavor. I played the cowardly lion, and several other adults and students filled the rest of the roles. It was a delight to perform this wonderful play.

As we study the characters amid the storyline, we can find many things that pertain to our lives. What was it that each of the main characters wanted? Dorothy, with her dog, Toto, had been whisked away by a tornado that had struck her house in Kansas. After her experiences in the Land of Oz, the thing she really wanted was to go back home. The scarecrow she encountered wanted a brain, the tin woodsman wanted a heart, and the cowardly lion wanted courage. Standing in their way were some challenges that are similar to the things we face today. The cyclone began it all, and throughout the journey Dorothy and her friends met with opposition—such as the poppies that put them all the sleep; the Wicked Witch of the West, with her evil minions, the flying monkeys; and their own insecurity about how to obtain their wishes.

Let us examine this story and see how it might apply to the things we desire out of life. This is a classic example of how a seemingly simple story can contain truths that can be applied to every individual. Once we have the tools to understand what life is about, we can apply them to help us overcome any obstacle that comes our way. A poem by R. L. Sharp, called "A Bag of Tools," includes this line: "Each is given a bag of tools, a shapeless mass, a book of rules; and each must make—ere life is flown—a stumbling block or a steppingstone."

We have examined what Dorothy and her friends want from the Wizard of Oz. As they journey there and finally come to the castle where the wizard lives, after the initial rejection, they are allowed to enter and confront the wizard. The wizard appears as a large, blustery fellow, with a deep voice that is loud and alarming. Dorothy introduces herself as meek and lowly, while her friends are cowering beside her. They all tell the wizard what they are seeking. Before the wizard is wont to grant any of their wishes, he sends them on a mission in which they will have to kill the Wicked Witch of the West. He tells them that upon their return he will grant them what they are seeking.

We know the story of their struggles and how they finally succeed in overcoming the Wicked Witch of the West. In that struggle, Scarecrow finds that he must use his brain to think of ways to help Dorothy overcome the evil witch. The Tin Woodsman finds that his great love for his friend Dorothy is enough to overcome the obstacles that are placed before him; he uses his heart to do anything that will save his friend. Cowardly Lion must also be willing to face grave danger, and he does so, using the courage that he has within him. He also learns that to be afraid in the face of such danger is normal, yet his actions prove that that is okay. Dorothy herself does not understand that the magic shoes she has are her chance to get back to her home. She merely has to click them together three times.

As the wizard grants them their wishes, Toto unveils what is behind the curtain—it is a mere man. So they learn that there really are no wizards, but that each of them has within the very thing that he or she desires.

As children of our heavenly father, we are given the gift of what is called free agency. This is the ability to make choices between good and bad, between right and wrong, to experience pleasure and pain, and to learn about blessings and consequences. We also know that each person is born with the Light of Christ, which we sometimes call the conscience. We were given the opportunity to come to this earth, willing to experience mortal life with all the challenges. So the key to understanding our agency is to know the proper way to live our lives in the context of biblical principles.

All of us have within ourselves a strand of spiritual DNA. The spirit we possess comes from our heavenly father. He loves us and wants us to return to him.

Let us begin with the war in heaven, in which Lucifer came up with a plan to force all of mankind to do his will, for which he wanted the glory of God. The plan that Christ offered was to allow men to choose for themselves. Satan was able to persuade one third of the host of heaven to take his side. Subsequently he was cast out to the earth, where he and his followers would never be allowed to obtain a physical body and gain exultation.

Since that time, there has been an attempt by Satan to persuade men to follow him using methods that appear to be legitimate. Some examples of Christ's plan versus Satan are these: in the place of prophecy by God's servants, Satan uses divination and fortune-telling. In place of the Spirit of God, there are evil spirits. In place of the priesthood, there is exorcism. In place of spiritual visions, there are hallucinations. In place of miracles and signs, there is magic in priestcraft. In place of prophets, there are mystics and false leaders. Finally, such devices as peep stones, Ouija boards, and black magic enter into the realm of falsity.

In reference to the light of Christ, president J. Reuben Clark, counselor in the First Presidency of The Church of Jesus Christ of Latter-Day Saints said, "Every human being is born with the light of faith kindled in his heart as on an altar, in that light burns, and the Lord sees that it burns, during the period before we are accountable. When accountability comes in, each of us determine how we shall feed and care for that light. If we live righteously, that life will glow until it suffuses the whole body, giving to it health and strength and spiritual light as well as bodily health. If we shall live on righteously, that light will dwindle and finally almost flicker out. It is my hope and my belief that the Lord never permits the light of faith holy to be extinguished in any human heart, however faint the light may glow. The Lord has provided that there shall be a spark which, with teaching, with the spirit of righteousness, with love, with tenderness, with example, with living the Gospel, shall brighten and glow again however darkened the mind may have been. And if we shall fail so to reach those among us of our own whose faith has dwindled low, we shall fail in one of the main things which the Lord expects at our hands." I also believe that this charge is carried by the missionaries of the Church of Jesus Christ of Latter-day Saints who go out into the world to teach all of God's children.

There are also two views about the nature of man and his relationship to God. I will outline some of the differences between these two views.

Theistic: God is supreme, and obedience to his will is a virtue. Personal identity is derived from the divine. Self-control requires a strict morality and obedience to religious ethics to define our relationship with God. Love and affection toward God and our fellow man is paramount, and service to others gives personal growth. Marriage between a man and woman, with complete fidelity and loyalty, is the Lord's way for his spirit children to be brought into the world. Personal responsibility for our own actions and accepting guilt with required repentance are the key changes needed in our lives. Forgiveness of others completes restoration of our own selves as we follow the Savior's admonition. Knowledge comes through faith and self-effort. Meaning and purpose in life are derived from spiritual insight.

Humanistic: Humans are supreme, and rejection of any external authority is good. Identity comes from the mortal realm, and relationships with others define self. Arguments for a flexible morality and situational ethics are advanced. Personal needs, including self-satisfaction, are central to one's growth. Open marriage, recreational sex, avoidance of long-term responsibilities, and self-gratification are presented as an alternative to God's plan. We can always blame others for things that happen to us and minimize our own personal responsibility. Knowledge comes by self-effort alone, and meaning and purpose are derived from reason and intellect.

We therefore need to apply the Scriptures to meet our everyday problems. They teach pure correct principles and contain the truths needed to keep us on the straight and narrow path. They also offer fundamental insights into the three basic elements of relationships: they identify the problem, determine the desired outcome, and allow each person a process to change his or her behavior. Whatever the problem, there is a remedy in the Scriptures.

As we look at the social, emotional, and spiritual strength of each individual, we can apply the gospel remedies to help provide the needed process to maximize our potential.

We are blessed to have modern-day prophets and apostles who can help us discover the prophetic destiny of the human race. There is a Scripture found in the book of Jacob within the book of Mormon, chapter 4 verse 13, which says, "He that prophesieth, let him prophesy to the understanding of men; for the Spirit speaketh the truth and lieth not. Wherefore, it speaketh of things as they really are, and other things as they really will be; wherefore, these things are manifested unto us plainly, for the salvation of our souls."

In our relationships with others, we can learn about love and its expression through sharing, friendship, service, concern, and caring. Through understanding we can learn to listen without making judgments and have empathy before drawing conclusions. Problem-solving is an art that requires us to assume responsibility in identifying the problem and working on its solution.

Finally, we know that one of the greatest powers in the world is the power of habit. We acquire both good and bad habits. Some of the good habits to acquire are efficient study habits, including reading and pondering the Scriptures for at least fifteen minutes a day. Work habits include the idea that there is no excellence without labor—this includes our mental capacity as well as our physical capacity. Thinking habits have a great influence on how we behave; positive and uplifting thoughts can help us overcome any temptation. Lastly, planning habits require that after we have studied, worked, thought about, and planned, we then proceed on our journeys to become better people, with an eye single to the glory of God.

We have learned that even a simple story like *The Wizard of Oz* can help us in our quest to make good moral decisions. We have it within ourselves to do so. It may take time, effort, and persistence to accomplish our goals, but they are certainly within our reach. We must understand the power that is within ourselves as children of God—this can move us toward our heavenly destination.

Example 1: Adam and Eve, our first parents, who used their agency to begin our mortal existence.

Example 2: Dorothy, the main character in *The Wizard of Oz*, who finally decided that there really is no place like home. The spiritual significance of that declaration should be an inspiration to all of us.

Scriptures: Genesis 2:16–17; Joshua 24:15; 2 Nephi 2:11; Doctrine and Covenants 37:4, 58:27–28.

About the Author

Richard Hanson grew up in the East and is a convert to the Church of Jesus Christ of Latter-day Saints along with his wife Nancy. They have 5 children and 10 grandchildren.

Richard (Dick) is a professional educator and has been a teacher, coach, counselor, and administrator at the K-12 level. He also taught a class at Brigham Young University and participated in one of the Education Week sessions.

He was a therapist and Director of the Veterans Administration Vet center in Provo, Utah where he offered services to Vietnam veterans. He served in Vietnam with the 1st Infantry Division where he was wounded and lost his right arm.

He has served as an Elders Quorum Pres., High Priest Group Leader, Branch Pres., Counselor in a District Presidency and Bishopric, and Gospel Doctrine Teacher.

Currently he serves as a home teacher and High Priest instructor in the Terreton, Idaho 2nd Ward. He and his wife Nancy are currently serving as missionaries for the Church of Jesus Christ of Latter-Day Saints at the Family History Center in Idaho Falls, Idaho.

He is the author of: "A Christian's Journey: A Modern Day Allegory". It is available at Lulu Press and Barnes and Noble. There is also a link on Facebook under Dick/Nancy Hanson.

He can be reached at hansonrr1@yahoo.com.

BIBLIOGRAPHY

1. Holy Bible The Church of Jesus Christ of Latter-day Saints Salt Lake City Utah Intellectual Reserve. Incorporated 2013.
2. The complete CS Lewis Signature Classics copyright by CS Lewis Pre. Ltd. 2002.
3. The Complete Grimm's Fairy Tales Pantheon Books copyright 1944 Random House Inc. New York.
4. Classical Education by Gene Edward Veith, Jr. and Andrew Kern Capital Research Center copyright 2001.
5. Never Before in History by Gary Amos and Richard Gardiner Foundation for Thought and Ethics, Richardson Texas copyright 1998.
6. Aesop's fables by Grosset and Dunlap 1973.
7. The great apostasy James E Talmadge Deseret Book Company Salt Lake City Utah 1909.
8. The American Tradition by Clarence B Carson Foundation for Economic Education, Inc. Irvington on Hudson, New York 1964.
9. The U.S. Constitution, A Reader Hillsdale College Press Hillsdale Michigan 2012.
10. The Founders Almanac edited by Matthew Spalding The Heritage Foundation Washington D.C. 2001.
11. McGuffey's Readers Van Nostrand Reinhold Revised Edition New York 1921.
12. The Best Loved Poems of the American People by Hazel Felleman Doubleday and Company Garden City Books New York 1936.
13. A Treasury of the Familiar Ralph L Woods, Editor McMillan Company Toronto, Canada 1969.
14. Poor Richard's Almanacks Ballantine Books division of Random House New York 1977.

Printed in the United States
By Bookmasters